Pelican Books
The Politics of Private Desires

Michael Laver was born in London in 1949 and
educated at Essex University. He then taught politics
at Queen's University, Belfast, and since 1973 has
been teaching politics at Liverpool University. His
previous publications include articles and
monographs on various aspects of politics, including
coalitions, party competition, electoral systems,
political loyalty, multinational corporations and
power, as well as lying, cheating and bluffing. He is
currently working on an analysis of strategic theories
of crime, and pursuing his interest in all aspects of
gaming. Penguin have also published *Playing
Politics* (1979).

Michael Laver

THE POLITICS
OF PRIVATE DESIRES

Penguin Books

Penguin Books Ltd, Harmondsworth,
Middlesex, England
Penguin Books, 625 Madison Avenue,
New York, New York 10022, U.S.A.
Penguin Books Australia Ltd, Ringwood,
Victoria, Australia
Penguin Books Canada Ltd, 2801 John Street,
Markham, Ontario, Canada L3R 1B4
Penguin Books (N.Z.) Ltd, 182–190 Wairau Road,
Auckland 10, New Zealand

First published 1981
Copyright © Michael Laver, 1981
All rights reserved

Set, printed and bound in Great Britain by
Cox & Wyman Ltd, Reading
Set in Linotype Juliana

Except in the United States of America, this book is
sold subject to the condition that it shall not, by
way of trade or otherwise, be lent, re-sold, hired out,
or otherwise circulated without the publisher's prior
consent in any form of binding or cover other than
that in which it is published and without a similar
condition including this condition being imposed on
the subsequent purchaser

Contents

Acknowledgements

The ideas discussed in this book owe much to the comments and criticisms of friends and colleagues. Many of these helpful suggestions have been wantonly ignored. Can I therefore simultaneously offer my thanks and my apologies to all of these people. (They know who they are, and if they don't, they won't mind being left out.) I must also thank those politicians whose behaviour reassured me when I sometimes began to doubt my assumptions. Brid Laver helped enormously by treating the whole thing with the contempt it probably deserves, yet (almost) voluntarily submitted herself to the extraordinary mental agony of listening to me reading the entire text aloud. I, of course, shoulder any blame that might be going.

Introduction

This book is about the political consequences of private desires. It presents an interpretation of the political world which is based on the assumption that people participate in politics in order to further their own private objectives. This is not quite as cynical as it might seem at first sight, since the whole endeavour is something of a mind game. I do not for one moment wish to suggest that selfish motivations are the only conceivable ones. They do represent, however, one of the many starting-points we can use in any attempt to expand our understanding of politics. I must also say that, in some societies at least, I find them quite a plausible starting-point.

The rules of this mind game are quite simple. Pretend, for the sake of argument, that people participate in politics entirely for reasons of self-interest, and try to discover what politics would look like if this were, indeed, the case. We construct an interpretation of politics using the assumption of self-interest as our foundation. If our construction looks rather like reality, this provides us only with some interesting food for thought. Even if we decide to accept that political participation is self-interested, we leave entirely open the question of why this might be. It is possible that people are inherently like this, but equally plausible that this is how they are conditioned. The arguments advanced in this book cannot, therefore, provide us with any *answers*; rather they ask questions. Their value is therefore largely heuristic. By directing us along certain logical paths, they may help us to understand our political processes and institutions a little better. Such arguments are aids to thought, concentrating the mind and producing, at most, interpretations, rather than explanations, of political reality.

This particular mind game has become a fashionable academic pastime over the past couple of decades. It is a pastime indulged in by a group of authors usually described as 'rational choice theorists'. This is actually rather a bad description, since the concept of rationality which they use has a special, technical, meaning. In common usage we usually praise someone by calling them rational, and criticize them by calling them irrational. The technical use of 'rationality', however, makes no such judgements. The label 'rational choice theory' is therefore confusing for all but the *cognoscenti*, but, like many confusing terms, is widely used. I would only compound matters by trying to change it, but please remember throughout that rationality has a special meaning. These 'theories' often intimidate the innocent bystander, borrowing extensively as they do from economics, and sometimes looking like a branch of applied mathematics. There is nothing inherently mathematical about them, however, although they do depend upon the more or less rigorous application of deductive logic to more or less precisely defined assumptions. I shall eschew mathematical formulations, in order to confine any brain-strain to the real issues and make the arguments as widely accessible as possible. There is really very little in the writing of these authors that is commonly stated in symbols and equations which cannot be expressed just as well in words and sentences. I use words and sentences throughout, and will take my chances with the purists. An occasionally distressing consequence of this is that the words and sentences are sometimes long and ugly, for which I apologize in advance.

The rational choice interpretation of politics comprises a collection of different 'theories' about different aspects of political life. The coy quotation marks which I am using indicate that these 'theories' are different from those with which most people will be familiar. The theories which we will consider are characterized by a deductive methodological style. In other words, they start with a set of *a priori* assumptions, definitions and concepts, which may or may not relate to the real world. These *a prioris* are manipulated logically in an attempt to do one of two things. Firstly, and in my view most importantly, they are manipulated in an attempt to produce either plausible or provocative interpretations of real politics. Secondly, they may be used to generate interesting hypotheses, which we can go out and test in (more or less) the normal way. As such, I do not think that these 'theories' are really theories at all in the commonly accepted sense. This is because most of the theories with which we are familiar are based on a process of induction, the logical manipulation of systematic statements about the world *as it actually is*. Thus, inductive theories attempt to explain what is actually going on. The ability to *predict* what will go on in the future is often used as a criterion by which to judge inductive theories, and may become an end in itself. In contrast to this, deductive theories, of which rational choice theories are a good example, attempt to provide us with ideas about what *would go on in certain circumstances*. Their primary function is to expand our understanding of the possibilities, rather than to explain events.

The logical manipulations engaged in by deductive theorists may be informal or formal, verbal or mathematical. The crucial characteristic is the generation of interesting and non-obvious statements about politics from a set of *a prioris* and a system of logic. In the strict sense of the word, therefore, rational choice theories should be tautological, entirely determined by the assumptions and the system of logic. The intellectual process involved is the logical unfolding of the implications of a particular set of assumptions. Readers should note that the word 'tautological' is commonly used as a term of abuse, rather than in its strict sense, often serving as a synonym for 'trivial' or 'boring'. Notwithstanding this, the purpose of rational choice theory is the search for *interesting and nontrivial* tautological arguments.

This means that the criteria for evaluating these writings are different from those used to judge a more conventional inductive theory. You may love or hate a particular deductive theory, but you will do so largely on the basis of what you think of its assumptions. If you find these assumptions interesting or stimulating, the logic sound, and the conclusions more than trivial, then you will find that the theories may increase your understanding. If you find the assumptions preposterous and pointless, the logic faulty, and the conclusions banal, then you will dismiss them out of hand.

While I strongly believe that this is the main criterion for evaluating these theories, they can nevertheless be used to generate 'testable' hypotheses. The interpretation of the results of this 'testing' is however, rather different, for deductive, as opposed to inductive, theories. If the logic of a deductive theory is sound, you will really be testing the accuracy of your *a priori* assumptions, since your hypotheses should ideally be tautologically generated from these. It should be clear that my own view is that the strict accuracy of the *a priori* assumptions is secondary to the heuristic value of the argument. Nevertheless, other things being equal, it is obviously useful to construct at least some of our deductive theories on the basis of plausible, rather than implausible, assumptions. I mentioned earlier that most of the ideas discussed in this book assume that political man is a selfish seeker of personal satisfaction. The primary objective is to understand what politics would look like if this were, indeed, the case. I also mentioned that I regarded this as, for whatever reasons, a not wholly implausible assumption upon which to base one interpretation of the politics of many western societies. This is a quite separate statement, and some light can be thrown on its validity if we test the hypotheses produced from our assumption of selfishness. (For example, we might predict that, other things being equal, electors will be more likely to vote the closer they live to the polling-booth, the better the weather, and the more important the election; see Chapter 4.)

Thus, the accounts of politics which we will be discussing are not pure speculation. They *can* be evaluated; their logic can be judged by the rules of logic, and their assumptions tested. Nevertheless, even if they provide us with no more than a basis for *interesting* speculation, I would argue that they are useful. To emphasize this point, I have confined my remarks on testing to an Appendix.

The rational choice approach therefore comprises a collection of different theories about various aspects of political life, held together by the methodological similarities we have just discussed. While these theories can take full advantage of the rigour and consistency provided by their deductive style as far as *internal* logic is concerned, any consistency *between* theories is largely fortuitous. Exhaustive, and occasionally exhausting, explorations of the full range of logical possibilities produced by a particular set of assumptions has often resulted in interesting and provocative conclusions about particular political processes. The sum total of all this endeavour is a collection of writers and writings which does, in practical terms, amount to a school, a paradigm, or a tradition. The problem is that, if we take each theory in turn and classify its premises and purpose, we find no obvious reason why they should all fit together.

For example, it does not take us long to identify a number of sub-species of *Homo politicus*. These range from the man in the jungle to the man in the street, to the voter, the party activist, the politician, the idealist and even, on occasion, the altruist. We might want to explain a particular process, such as turning out to cast a vote at elections. We see that the voter receives little in return for the expenditure made in terms of shoe leather, time and mental distress, and we therefore invoke such motivations as 'the satisfaction of complying with the ethic of voting' or 'civic duty'.[1] In contrast, when explaining other forms of participation, such as belonging to a trade union or a consumer group, we scratch our heads and puzzle about the 'collective action problem', when invoking 'civic duty' might solve the problem at a stroke.

In order to reconcile the various rational choice theories, I shall attempt to describe them in the following chapters as if they had all been deduced from a common set of 'core' assumptions. Much more controversially, I am going to apply a very rigid criterion to the assumptions which I will allow into this core set. This is that I shall include only those assumptions about the motivations of individuals which can be precisely defined with reference to a single individual, as opposed to a collection of individuals. In short, I will allow only asocial assumptions about the motivations of individuals. The set of core assumptions will therefore resemble a 'state of nature' in some ways. The state-of-nature technique is undergoing a minor renaissance following the publication of recent works by Robert Nozick and John Rawls.[2] It is, in my view, a very useful method of ensuring that, whatever their plausibility, the deductive theories we consider produce accounts of the political realm which are not trivial. While state-of-nature methodology is not an integral part of the deductive method itself, it provides a very powerful criterion for maintaining the distinction between deductive and inductive styles of argument. Nozick's methodological assertion, and it is no more than an assertion, is that this approach enables us to generate 'fundamental potential explanations' of the political realm. These explanations are fundamental in the sense that they are based on assumptions defined in a different realm from the realm of the process to be explained, and potential in the sense that, if the *assumptions* were correct and the logic sound, they would be accurate explanations of what was going on. The explanation is interesting, even if the assumptions are found to be untenable, since

> We learn much by seeing how the state could have arisen, even if it didn't arise that way. If it didn't arise that way, we would also learn much by determining why it didn't: by trying to explain why the particular bit of the real world that deviates from the state-of-nature model is as it is.[3]

The implicit assumption in this argument is that explanations of phenomena in one realm (the political), on the basis of motivational assumptions defined entirely in another realm (the individual), are somehow 'deeper' than explanations of the political in terms only of the political. While I am not totally convinced by this, I am convinced that the *heuristic* value of deductive explanations is greatly enhanced if this canon is observed, since it greatly reduces the danger of triviality which haunts all tautological arguments. Without wishing to give too much away at this stage, an example might clarify the point. Consider an interpretation of participation in politics which might be produced by a rational choice theorist. We set out to explain participation, and begin by asking the question 'why'. Why do people participate? Because they want to. Why do they want to? Because they have been conditioned to do so. Why are they conditioned to do so? A rational choice theorist might say, 'Because those who engage in the conditioning process have learnt or worked out that if they do not participate, both the person giving and the person receiving the conditioning will not get what they privately want. This is because they both privately want certain things which can only be produced as a result of public participation.' This would be a (very general) fundamental potential explanation of public participation. The questions we want to ask come to an end, and we feel that we have got somewhere by moving from one realm to another. The point at which we feel the explanation has achieved something is the point at which our explanation maps statements defined in one realm into statements defined in another.

An alternative method of confronting the same problem would be to adopt a quite different, and more inductive, style. We would observe the characteristics which appeared to be related to participation, and try to make some sense out of these relationships. If a perfect piece of empirical research could be conducted on this subject, it could quite possibly provide a perfectly plausible and interesting inductive account of public participation. This account might even enable us to predict participation patterns in future events, and, in its own terms, would be an eminently respectable piece of work. This approach would not, however, enable us to explore all the possibilities, the prime virtue of the deductive approach. The inductive explanation *in the last analysis* more or less says that the world is as it is because that is how it is. Much emphasis is therefore placed on empirical investigation, although inductive theory would not be theory at all without interesting and plausible explanations of the relationship between the various component parts of the whole to be explained. The deductive explanation tells us how the world might be, when the world might be one of a number of things. Empirical observation is of limited usefulness, and must therefore be replaced with something else upon which to base our conclusions. My argument is that empirical observation must be replaced with a set of fundamental *a priori* motivational assumptions, defined in the individual realm, if we are to achieve anything interesting by way of a deductive explanation of the political.

I regard the clinching argument in favour of the use of fundamental potential explanations, or something like them, to be the need to maintain a clear distinction between inductive and deductive modes of explanation. It is clear that these alternative modes of explanation should not be employed simultaneously. If, in the same account of politics, we alternate deductive and inductive analyses, we will greatly undermine the value of our explanation, reducing it to little more than a rationalization of the world as it actually is. A number of rational choice theorists have fallen into this trap, starting with a set of *a priori* motivational assumptions arriving at a point where their deductions seriously diverge from observed reality, and solving their problems at a stroke by switching into the inductive mode. They modify their *a prioris* in such a way as to allow them to deduce observed reality, and proceed blithely on their way as if nothing at all had happened. If we do this, we can explain absolutely anything. This is very convenient but rather unsatisfying, since rational choice theory becomes little more than the rationalization of choice. The use of fundamental potential explanations does not, of course, automatically eliminate this possibility, but it does serve two useful functions. In the first place, it makes the analyst more aware of what is being attempted at each stage of the explanatory process. Furthermore, it is often the case that the introduction of new, socially defined, *a prioris* is the most tempting and damaging response for a deductive analyst faced with a divergence between theory and reality.

It is important to notice that I am not claming that 'the social whole is no more than the sum of its individual parts'. While I shall insist that fundamental *motivational* assumptions are defined entirely in terms of isolated individuals, secondary motivational assumptions, such as the desire to participate, may be deduced from these, and may make sense only in terms of a group of individuals. Furthermore, many of the definitions and concepts used will only make sense when applied to collectivities. Much of the discussion in this book, for example, is concerned with the concept of public goods. If there was only one individual in the whole world, the concept of public goods would make no sense, since public goods are things which individuals privately desire, but which can be consumed only collectively. The theories which I discuss, therefore, are not totally reductionist, although they come quite close to being so; we should be under no illusions about that. The many disadvantages of reductionist methodologies must be acknowledged, and offset against the advantages which can be gained from them, in heuristic terms as well as in terms of increased coherence and rigour. At this level, all rational choice theories are necessarily reductionist in their attempt to deduce explanations of the political process from assumptions about individual motivations. The rather strict approach adopted in this book therefore presents no new problems in this respect. It merely represents an attempt to extract the maximum advantage in exchange for the inevitable short-comings of this methodology.

Rational choice theorists have written about many aspects of politics, including party competition, voting, coalitions, collective action, bargaining, international relations, military and nuclear strategy, and so on. This book is in no sense a review of the litera-ture. It is an attempt to construct a coherent argument from a selection of these writings which might prove one interpretation of competition in the modern political system. It is bound, therefore, to be highly idiosyncratic, and I make no apologies for this.

A central theme of the book will be the various means by which public goods may be provided to a group of rational individuals. The nature of public goods is discussed in the first chapter, in which the core assumptions are also defined. In the second chapter, we move on to consider the problems created by public goods provision. This is a mainstream concern of rational choice theorists, and is usually referred to as the 'collective action problem'. (Economists discuss it more in terms of 'market failure'.) The collective action problem defines the central paradox generated by our indi-vidualistic motivational assumptions. If a group of people behave so as to maximize their individual welfare, they produce a state of affairs which is worse for each of them, individually, than one which would have been produced if they had adopted more cooper-ative behaviour. This paradox is so fundamental that it has even been presented by some as a major justification for the role of the state, which is seen as necessary in order to force people to cooperate 'for their own good'. At this stage, it can easily be seen why some of modern rational choice theory has taken on a de-cidedly neo-Hobbesian flavour. The state fulfils, for some authors, a role which is rather like that of the Hobbesian sovereign, bringing about peace rather than a war of all against all. There are import-ant differences between the two positions, however, which are dis-cussed in Chapter 2; most of these relate to differences in the fundamental assumptions made by Hobbes and by rational choice theorists.

The problem of public goods provision has had some interesting consequences, however, since it can reconcile even the most hard-core proponents of a minimalist state to the need for state intervention in certain spheres of social life. In Chapter 2, we also explore the anarchist argument that public goods may be produced, in certain circumstances, without state intervention. The 'certain circumstances' in which this solution works are very much those which we might expect to be preconditions for an anarchist system. Groups of individuals must be small, members must be relatively far-sighted, and have relatively equal access to resources, and must mainly desire public goods involving the modification of their behaviour, rather than large-scale collective investment of resources. This suggests that, by doing considerable violence to the spirit of the various authors' arguments, we can represent the anarchist 'solution' as an interpretation of the way in which certain goods involving behaviour modification are produced, even within a modern state. Adherence to norms and values, for example, is rarely enforced by governments, but does provide valuable public benefits which can be privately enjoyed by many people. Thus, there is no law which compels us to wait in line at bus queues, but we all 'anarchistically' agree to do this, even on those occasions when we might want to barge in at the front. We already regulate large areas of our social life along 'anarchistic' lines.

An alternative solution to the problem of public goods provision may be provided by a political entrepreneur, who supplies these goods at a profit, provided that he or she can overcome the problem of how to raise the necessary revenue for a good which all can consume, whether they contribute or not. Political entrepreneurs are much less written about by rational choice theorists, despite the fact that they are one of the basic actors in any system of party competition, and despite the fact that party competition is a mainstream concern of these authors. Our discussion, in Chapter 3, of these entrepreneurs, and the ways in which they must realize a surplus, suggests a major revision of conventional theories of party competition. This revision places more emphasis on the influence of campaign financing on the policies of political parties. Conventional rational choice theory presents political parties as unitary actors, but the approach adopted in this book is to deduce their role as coalitions of entrepreneurs attempting to realize a surplus from public goods provision. Conventional rational choice theory represents the prime motivation of parties as being to maximize votes, rather than to maximize the surplus realized from entrepreneurial public goods provision. Voters are only one source of this revenue, to which the suppliers of the 'factors of production' of the public goods also contribute. The preferences of these suppliers will play a major role, therefore, in the particular public goods packages advocated by the competing parties. The implications of this, and of the behaviour of voters, are explored in Chapters 4 and 5.

Finally, in Chapter 6, we look at the formation of coalitions between political parties in those circumstances where no single party controls an overall majority. Once more, theories of coalition formation illustrate an odd omission in the work of most rational choice theorists. While 'coalition theory' itself is one of the boom industries in the discipline, rational choice theories of party competition and rational choice theories of coalition formation have been developed with little regard for one another. Yet it is clearly the case that the structure of coalition bargaining will play an important part in competition between rational politicians, and *vice versa*. The primary focus of the chapter on coalitions, therefore, is not coalition theory, about which much has been written, but the interaction between coalition formation and party competition.

Overall, therefore, the intention of this book is to present part of rational choice theory as a coherent whole, rather than as a selection of disparate writings. I have found that the most interesting consequence of this endeavour has been the need to produce sometimes rather substantial revisions of various theories in order to fit them together. The most critical phase of the argument is almost certainly the reconciliation of public goods theory with theories of party competition, and it is here that I find the revisions of the existing theories most interesting. The most problematic phase of the argument concerns the behaviour of voters in large electorates.

I have a feeling that this reflects the relative unsuitability of the rational choice approach to explanation of most forms of mass behaviour, a theme to which I will return in my conclusions.

1 Rational Man

We begin with two fundamental categories: men and goals. All men are not considered to be equal; neither are some considered to be more equal than others. Goals are the things that men want.

We start the argument by considering a single man in isolation from his fellows. He will be assumed at the outset to possess only those desires which make sense when defined in terms of an isolated unique individual. This means that any 'socially' defined goals which he might possess, such as power, prestige and glory, will be ignored for the time being. Such socially defined goals make sense only when applied to a *collection* of individuals, and have no meaning in relation to a single individual, viewed in complete isolation from all others. 'Rational' men are motivated by the desire to realize goals. This very general definition requires more detailed specification when considered in conjunction with our first serious proposition. This is that *the goals that men desire are in short supply*.

At the most basic level, even Eve, the only girl in the world, cannot have everything she wants. Nature sees to that. She might want to walk on water, but that would be just too bad. The realization of goals by an individual involves the expenditure of resources. Each individual is vested by nature (or God) with a limited stock of such resources. These resources are denominated, in their most basic form, in terms of physical and mental capacity, such as strength, energy, endurance, determination and intelligence. Different resources obviously have very different properties, and the limits to physical and mental resources take various forms. Some limits are absolute and immutable – for example, the amount of time available in one day. Other limits are absolute, but within the control of the individual – for example, the amount of information stored in the brain. Some resources, such as time and energy, are expendable, while others, such as information and intelligence, are not. The expenditure of some resources, such as energy, is within the control of the individual; the expenditure of other resources, such as time, is not.

These limits to, and constraints on, the stock of resources available for realizing goals mean that, for each individual, the set of goals which can be realized is only a subset of the universe of all possible goals. Given these limits, some potential goals will be unrealizable under any circumstances. For the individual concerned, these goals can be thought of as intrinsically unrealizable. Thus, the desires to fly unassisted and to walk on water are intrinsically unrealizable for nearly all human beings, given the particular stock of resources available to them. For birds and pond-skaters, having different stocks of resources, limitations on the set of realizable goals will of course be different.

Other goals, while not *intrinsically* unrealizable, cannot be fully realized with a given stock of resources. Eve may like truffles and want a million tons of them. While she could expend some resources in acquiring some truffles, she could never accumulate a million tons of truffles in her whole lifetime (even if that many exist). The desire for truffles, unlike the desire to walk on water, can be realized. Nevertheless, truffles will be in short supply, since it is possible to desire more of them than can be realized with any given stock of resources.

So far, we have considered only one desire at a time. Individuals, however, will want lots of different things. It is quite possible that a collection of goals will contain several elements which are mutually incompatible. Either one of a pair of desires may be realizable on its own, but it may be impossible to realize both desires together. Thus, Eve may want a perfect physique (body), and at the same time she may want to spend her whole life asleep (bed). She cannot gratify both desires and must therefore choose between them. Neither goal is, on its own, in short supply, but a package containing both body and bed is unrealizable, because the two goals are incompatible. Some sets of goals which are not *intrinsically* incompatible may be mutually exclusive, given a particular stock of resources. Eve may want a small sack of truffles and a ton of fillet steak. While she can have each on its own, she may well not possess enough time, energy, intelligence and whatever else it takes to realize both of these desires in her own lifetime.

To sum up, realizing goals involves expending resources, and each individual is endowed with a limited stock of resources. This limited stock of resources constrains the realization of goals by rendering some absolutely unobtainable and some partially unobtainable, and by rendering some *sets* of goals incompatible. Only individuals with completely compatible sets of goals, which can all be fully realized with the stock of available resources, will find that goals are not in short supply.

CHOOSING BETWEEN GOALS

At any point in time, each individual will be faced with a choice between a number of different courses of action. These courses of action will involve the commitment of different amounts of different types of resource. Different courses of action will therefore have different consequences for the achievement of goals. Faced with a choice between courses of action, a rational individual must be able to choose the course of action which realizes his or her set of goals most effectively. In order to do this, the individual must be able to choose between the sets of goals which are the probable outcome of alternative courses of action. Before making such a choice, the individual must, at the very least, be able to place various desired goals in some sort of order of preference. If Eve is faced with a choice between two courses of action, one of which yields more truffles, while the other yields more fillet steak, she must decide which of these goals she most prefers before she can decide which course of action to take.

Placing goals in an order of preference is a start, but will not enable a rational individual to choose the best course of action in all circumstances. Actions have consequences for *sets* of goals, and one course of action may yield one set of goals, while an alternative course of action yields a set which contains some elements which are better, and some elements which are worse, than those in the first set. If Eve places four of her goals in the order truffles, body, steak and bed, one action may produce truffles and bed, while another action produces body and steak. Simply knowing the *order* in which she prefers her various goals does not help her, in this case, to make a rational choice between the two courses of action. One course of action yields her top and her bottom preference, while the other yields her middle two choices. She must decide *how much* she prefers truffles to body to steak to bed before she can make a decision. She needs, in other words, to assign *values* to her various goals. These values, or 'cardinal utilities', will enable her to decide between alternative sets of goals, when one set does not clearly dominate the other as an unequivocally superior alternative.

Another circumstance in which a rational individual will need to consult the cardinal utilities associated with various goals is when faced with a choice between courses of action which yield *risky* outcomes. When, for a given expenditure of resources, one action yields one goal with a certain probability, while an alternative action yields a different goal with a different probability, simply deciding which of the two goals is preferred will not enable a rational choice to be made between the two courses of action. A rational decision-maker would be forced to consider the value of the alternative outcomes, together with their probabilities. The chosen course of action would be the one yielding the highest expected value. Expected values can, of course, only be calculated on the basis of cardinal utilities. If Eve prefers truffles to fillet steak, and she knows that one course of action gives her a 20 per cent chance of truffles and an 80 per cent chance of nothing, while an alternative course of action gives her a 90 per cent chance of fillet steak and a 10 per cent chance of nothing for the same expenditure of resources, she cannot decide what she should do unless she can assign values to both. The higher the value she attaches to truffles relative to steak, the greater the risks she will be prepared to take in order to have some chance of ending up with truffles. Conversely, if she hardly prefers truffles at all, then a good chance of ending up with steak will look a lot more attractive than a long shot at some of these delectable and exotic fungi.

The characterization of rational man as a 'maximizer of cardinal utility' is a common elaboration of the definition of rational man as a seeker of goals. The concept of utility provides the means to enable the efficient realization of desires. It should be emphasized at this point that nothing at all has been said about the nature of these desires. In other words, it is still assumed that Eve may derive utility from absolutely anything, even from being run over by a steam-roller or diving head first into an empty swimming-pool. We will refer to this position later on as the completely unrestricted definition of rationality. Most contemporary definitions describe rationality as goal-directed behaviour, often go on to specify this in terms of cardinal preference orderings, but are always very careful to refrain from specifying any *particular* type of goal as 'more rational' than any other. Rationality is seen as trying to get what you want, *whatever* that may be.[1]

Thus far, we have considered only goals which mean values *intrinsically*; goals which are valued for their own sake. We now assume that, in addition to these, individuals may have a set of goals which are not valued *in themselves*, but rather because they can *help to achieve* intrinsically valued goals. For example, if Eve is thirsty, she can lie on her back with her mouth wide open when it rains. This will not be a very efficient way of quenching her thirst. She may decide that some form of water-collector, such as a bucket, will gather much more rainwater in less time. This will leave her not only with more to drink, but with more resources available to her to realize other goals. She will value the bucket, not because she has any intrinsic desire to possess one, but because it helps her to maximize her well-being.

Goals which are valued only because they help to realize other goals are 'instrumental' goals. The analytical classification of goals into instrumental and intrinsic goals is, of course, simply a definitional exercise. In practice, many goals will be both intrinsic and instrumental. Eve may value good health, for example, because it enables her to capture and consume all sorts of other goodies, as well as because she derives intrinsic satisfaction from being healthy. For each individual, each goal will have some intrinsic and some instrumental value.

We must make one further assumption in order to proceed. Thus far, we have considered only the *benefits* of one course of action relative to another, but it is clear that the process of deciding between courses of action will itself be costly. Decision costs will include the opportunity costs of the time consumed, the resource costs of gathering the necessary information, and any other investment of resources involved in actually deciding what to do. These costs are very important, since it may not be rational to even consider taking certain decisions, if the costs of deciding outweigh the probable benefits of deciding correctly. Thus, if a sack of truffles is sitting on top of a lake covered in thin ice, considerable resources might be expended in order to decide upon the best route, since the costs of the wrong decision would be large. If the same sack of truffles was in the middle of a dry grassy meadow, while it is still true that one route to the truffles might be better than another, most routes will be so similar that any costs in deciding upon the best would almost certainly be wasted. Thus, a rational individual may well opt for a course of action in the knowledge that something better probably exists, having decided that it is not worth spending resources to decide what that something actually is.

Such behaviour is a form of what is sometimes referred to in the literature as 'satisficing'. There are a number of definitions of satisficing, most of which involve a modification of the utility-maximizing definition of rational action.[2] I do not intend to make such a serious modification to the definition, however, and will consider the conscious adoption of a course of action, which is known to be less cost-effective than another, to be irrational. However, the conscious adoption of a course of action when it *might* be less cost-effective than another, in those circumstances when settling this question involves the investment of more resources than the best estimate of the difference in utility income at stake, *is* consistent with our unmodified definition, and might be thought of as satisficing. Thus I devote much more effort to deciding upon which car to buy than I do upon which box of matches. Even if I know that a particular brand of matches is hopeless, I will rationally buy it anyway, since shopping around is not worth it.

To summarize, an isolated rational individual will try to realize goals which are effectively in short supply. This will involve placing goals in an order of preference and, usually, assigning precise values to them. These precise utilities will facilitate decisions between risky courses of action, and between alternative sets of goals in those circumstances in which one set of goals does not clearly dominate the other. Some elements in any particular set of goals will be intrinsically valued; others will be valued mainly because they are instrumental to the realization of intrinsically valued goals.

MORE MEN

We have so far considered the behaviour of each rational inhabitant of our universe as if no one else in the world existed. Consider a universe populated by more than one rational individual. Each individual may have a completely different set of goals, both intrinsic and instrumental. If this is the case, then no individual will come into conflict with any other. If rational individuals share some goals in common, however, the possibility emerges that some individuals will be able to realize their goals, but that all individuals will not. Goals which are not in short supply with respect to a single individual will be in short supply if they are shared as goals by a group of individuals. Even in the wilderness, biological similarities between individual members of the same species will ensure that some, at least, of their goals are held in common. Furthermore, there will be a set of goals which are in short supply for individuals, but which are in even shorter supply when desired by a group of individuals. In these circumstances, rational individuals will find themselves in a state of *potential* competition with each other over the realization of goals.

It is clear that this competition will not only concern intrinsically valued goals, but also extend to the instrumental means to acquire these. A direct consequence of potential competition is that people will seek to prevent others from realizing those goals which they themselves desire, and will furthermore be able to realize goals by expropriating them from others, rather than by expropriating them directly from nature. Potential competition therefore provides a justification for important new types of instrumental goal. These will be the various aids to resisting encroachment from others, to preventing others from realizing valued goals, and to expropriating goals from others rather than directly from nature. These instrumental means of attack and defence can be thought of as weapons. Weapons can be both physical and psychological. The *physical* value of an enormous spikey club is obvious. Consider, however, a particular individual who had destroyed all previous opponents with an enormous spikey club. The successful and ruthless use of this physical weapon over a period of time will create certain expectations on the part of potential competitors and likely victims, perhaps discouraging them from going anywhere near the club-wielder. It may even become unnecessary to wield the club at all, as potential competitors flee when this beclubbed silhouette looms on the horizon. A reputation for violence would achieve the same effect as the violence itself. This reputation would be a sort of psychological weapon, valued instrumentally since it would greatly assist the owner in gathering all sorts of other goodies. An individual could develop such a reputation by going around clubbing all and sundry, whether or not they were likely to be rivals, simply in order to become known as a hard case.

Thus, the general set of instrumental goals will contain an important subset, consisting of those goals which become necessary because of the competition between rational individuals over intrinsic and instrumental goals which are in short supply. A significant subset of this set of weapons will be socially defined.

At this point, it is important to re-emphasize one of the major implications of the methodological style of this argument. We are dealing with fundamental potential explanations of the political realm, and therefore must be careful to ensure that the motivational assumptions we make about individuals are essentially *asocial* in character. A rational individual in a group will develop all sorts of instrumental goals, arising from conflict and cooperation with others over the realization of intrinsically valued goals. These goals are 'socially defined', in the sense that a socially defined goal is incapable of definition with reference to a single individual living in total isolation from all others. Socially defined goals include power, esteem, respect, the urge to be feared, liked, envied and so on. The use of fundamental potential explanations demands that we make a further crucial assumption. This is that socially defined goals have no *intrinsic* value for the individual and are desired solely for *instrumental* reasons. This critical assumption is the engine which gives us intellectual lift-off, and provides the distinctive character of rational choice theory. The statement that rational man is a maximizer of utility is insufficient in itself to achieve this, if we allow utility to be derived from absolutely anything. If any action can be rational (because there will always be some goal which it furthers), our core assumptions are insufficiently constrained to generate more than truisms. In contrast, eliminating the possibility of socially defined intrinsic goals provides a very strong constraint and considerable analytical purchase. It is this, rather than any statement about utility-maximization, which enables us to make non-trivial deductions. The character of rational choice theory is thus defined firstly by an assumption that man is a utility-maximizing decision-maker, and secondly by an assumption that the goals from which utility is *ultimately* derived are essentially asocial in character. The point of the whole endeavour is to take certain (socially defined) political goals and to attempt to construct fundamental potential explanations of them. Rational choice theories which do not employ these, or equivalent, constraints are doomed to triviality.

THE SOCIAL CONTEXT OF GOALS

Any consideration of the problems faced by an individual, who must coexist with others who share subsets of his or her set of goals, must involve a discussion of the distinctive social properties of various types of goal. These social properties can be ignored by an individual who does not interact with others, for whom everything is private. When rational people coexist, however, they will quickly become aware of the social context of many of their goals. Two fundamental properties of goals in this respect concern the manner of their realization, or production, and the manner of their enjoyment, or consumption.

The social context of consumption forms the basis of a distinction between private consumption goods and public, or collective, consumption goods.[3] When an individual consumes a 'private' consumption good, he appropriates the whole of the benefit of that good for himself. Thus, a perfect example of a private consumption good is food. The consumption by one individual of a particular piece of food makes it considerably less attractive (as food) to others.

The polar opposite of a private consumption good is a public consumption good. This is a good 'which all enjoy in common in the sense that each individual's consumption of such a good leads to no subtraction from any other individual's consumption of that good'.[4] The set of goods cannot, however, simply be divided into those which are private and those which are public. Between those polar extremities lies a continuum of 'publicness'.[5] This continuum has four component characteristics, each of which contributes to the publicness of any given good. These are the 'jointness or divisibility of supply', the 'excludability', the 'optionality' and the 'susceptibility to crowding' exhibited by the good in question.[6]

We have defined a 'private' good as one for which all of the utility arising from consumption accrues to one individual. Obviously, that individual therefore *crowds* all the others out of potential consumption of the good. Consider a typical 'collective' consumption good, such as a lighthouse. Use of the lighthouse by one individual does not leave any less lighthouse around for others to consume. Indeed, (almost) any number of people can use a lighthouse, and they will wear it out no more than if no one used it. In dire extremes, vast numbers of users might crowd the lighthouse at any particular time, making it impossible for anyone else to even get a glimpse of it. By and large, however, lighthouses will not be susceptible to crowding. Other goods will not be purely private, but will be susceptible to some crowding. A public park, for example, may be used by a fair number of people with no subtraction from anyone else's enjoyment. There will come a point when the addition of any more consumers reduces the enjoyment of others, because the park is becoming crowded. Obviously, very small public parks might be very susceptible to crowding, but they are clearly not private goods. (A public park capable of holding only one person would, however, be like a private good in this respect.) A fantastically large public park, such as the Sahara Desert, may take quite a lot of crowding. The less susceptible to crowding a good is, the more public it is, because the less its use by one individual restricts its use by others.

Some goods are forced on their consumers, while in other cases the consumer has the choice of whether to consume it or not. Thus individuals may choose whether or not to consume a public park, but cannot choose whether or not to consume the collective defence of the island they inhabit. If the collective defence of the island is consumed at all, it is consumed by all its inhabitants, *whether they want to or not.* Obviously, something which is regarded as a good by one individual may be regarded as a bad by someone else. Thus the more optional a good is, the more private it is, since the smaller the probability that an individual will be forced to consume something that is viewed as a bad. The less optional a good is, the more public. The degree of 'optionality' may be measured in terms of the costs to an individual of voluntary self-exclusion from consumption of the good. It costs nothing to exclude yourself from the consumption of a public park, but it costs an enormous amount to exclude yourself from the collective defence of your country. Excluding yourself from the loud music emitted by your neighbour may involve some modest cost to you as you make your own loud music to drown the din, or give up and go out drinking.

If consumption of a good is absolutely unavoidable, then it is obviously impossible to exclude specified individuals from consuming it. If a good is optional, however, this might or might not be possible. It is very easy to exclude specified individuals from a public park, but almost impossible to exclude them from a beautiful sunset, despite the fact that both goods are entirely optional. At any cost, of course, it is possible to exclude almost anyone from almost anything. Enormous screens could be built to obscure the sunset, but these would be very expensive. While people might pay to see the sunset if you could control access, they would probably never pay you enough to cover the cost of gaining that control, in this case the costs of building the screens. In general, exclusion may involve the expenditure of more resources than can be recouped as a direct consequence of being able to control access to the good in question. Thus sunsets are effectively not excludable, while public parks are, since it is easy to put gates or guards around a park, and likely that people would pay a high enough entry fee for exclusion costs to be recovered. The degree of 'excludability' is thus measured by the costs involved in exclusion, relative to the benefits. Goods will tend to be excludable or not in a given context, depending upon whether the exclusion costs can be recouped.

Finally, the more public a good is, the more likely it is to be 'jointly supplied'. Jointly supplied goods must be available for consumption in equal quantities by all members of a group, if they are available for consumption at all by any members of the group. (Note that membership of this group may be flexible if the good is excludable.)[7] A purely private good is perfectly divisible, and can thus be supplied in any mix of quantities to any mix of people. A jointly supplied good is made available in the same quantity to all consumers. The small public park is a jointly supplied good, despite the fact that it is susceptible to crowding, while the lighthouse is a jointly supplied good which cannot be crowded. Collective security, however, may be differentially available to different inhabitants of an island, if defences at some points are stronger than defences elsewhere. People living near the strongly defended points may receive more security than others. Thus, collective security is not necessarily jointly supplied, although it is very public in most other respects, being non-optional, non-crowdable and non-excludable. A small public park is jointly supplied, despite the fact that it is relatively optional, crowdable and excludable.

Publicness of supply thus has four components. Increasing one or more of the optionality, crowdability, excludability and divisibility of a good makes it more private, while any decrease in one of these components makes consumption of the good more public. Since publicness is a continuum, all goods which are not absolutely private will be to a certain extent public. Conventionally, however, goods are usually described as public consumption goods if they are jointly supplied and if it is not cost-effective to exclude people from their consumption.

The second social property of goals concerns the method of their realization, or production. Many goals can be realized by an individual acting in total isolation. These include, for example, the harvesting of basic foodstuffs, and the provision of rudimentary shelter and entertainment. At the opposite extreme, there are sets of goals which can only be realized by groups of individuals acting in concert, even if each individual possessed infinite resources. Examples of this can be found in any endeavour, such as the climbing of a very difficult rock face, which would require the same individual to be simultaneously in a number of different places. Such a good intrinsically involves 'joint production' if it is ever to be realized at all.

Between these extremes lies a whole range of goals which can, in principle at least, be produced independently by an isolated individual, but can be much more efficiently and economically realized when individuals act in concert. Thus, while an isolated Robinson Crusoe might trap a few wild animals on his own, organized bands of hunters can realize vast increases in productivity, as anyone who has tried to encircle a herd of wild elephants single-handed will know. Thus, in addition to the set of goals which simply cannot be realized by an isolated individual, there is another set yielding joint gains from economies of scale, trade, division of labour and so on.

We can easily see from the previous examples that publicness of consumption and publicness of production are two analytically separate properties of particular goals. Collective consumption goods which can be efficiently produced on a purely private basis present no problems. As long as the production of these goods yields a private surplus, rational individuals will produce them, despite the fact that the benefits can be enjoyed by others. Thus, someone deeming the likely benefits of a potential discovery or innovation worth the investment of private resources will invest those resources anyway, and disregard the benefits which others might reap from this investment. Similarly, someone who enjoys making beautiful music will do so despite the 'free' benefits to others. They might wish that they could charge others for these benefits, but, if the good is purely public so that it cannot be withheld from nonpayers, they will not modify their research or musical activity to spite free-riders. Formally, this private production would yield public externalities. In this case, the externalities (knowledge or music) are likely to be positive, so that public goods are created. Frequently, public externalities to private production are negative, as in the case of pollution.

Conversely, there are many private consumption goods which can only be effectively produced collectively. Indeed, when we consider *sets* of private consumption goods, as opposed to the individual elements of a set, the gains to be realized by joint production will almost always be manifest. Collections of individuals, each endowed with different amounts of different types of resource, facing different environmental constraints, and desiring different sets of goals, will almost invariably find that they can realize gains from trade. Trade is one means of coordinating the joint production of sets of private goals, to take advantage of efficient divisions of labour, or economies of scale and so on.

The most serious problems arise over the *joint production of goods which are collectively consumed.* Consider a group of people locked in a small room, all pathological smokers, but all aware that, if they all smoke, the air will quickly become unbreathable. The air in the room is collectively consumed, since it will be in the same state for all who breathe it. If one person smokes, all must breathe the smoky air. Clean air in the room is therefore jointly produced, since no individual acting on his own – unless he has a machine gun – can produce it. If one person smoking does not make much difference, then clean air will be very difficult to produce in that room, as each pathological smoker wants to reap the benefits of clean air without contributing to the costs.

Similarly, we have already seen how rational men will desire weapons of offence and defence. Yet the investment of resources in weapons of offence and defence is not an intrinsically productive activity. Such resources are wasted in the same sense that, if no weapons existed, people would be able instead to devote their resources exclusively to expropriating goals from nature. The group, *as a whole*, would be better off if all members agreed to disarm. Any individual would be better off, however, allowing the others to disarm, then appearing with an enormous spikey club and expropriating everything in sight. It is unlikely that anyone in the group would expose themselves to this risk, so that all will be forced to continue expending resources on weapons. This is because group disarmament is both a joint consumption good and a joint production good. All can enjoy some of the benefits of disarmament, whether they disarm or not, yet disarmament cannot be produced at all unless a number of people cooperate.

The collective security brought about by unanimous multilateral disarmament is an example of a good requiring pure jointness of production, since it is impossible to produce it at all without the participation of every member of the group. It will be more common, however, for goods to be jointly produced because the investments involved would not be cost-effective for a single individual. Thus, rational sailors may want a lighthouse, but no single rational sailor would want one if he or she had to pay for it single-handed. In such cases, an individual's participation in the production process will often amount to no more than the contribution of resources towards the costs of production. Often, any individual contribution might not be at all critical to the production of the good, so that the expected value of the good for a single consumer is unrelated to the participation of that consumer. Our group of rational sailors would have to be quite large, for example, for them to contemplate building themselves a lighthouse. Any sailor in this large group would know that his or her contribution would almost certainly make no perceivable difference to the value of the lighthouse. Thus, since it can be used by all and sundry, whether or not those who consume have also contributed, rational sailors will not contribute. The consequence of this, of course, will be that this splendid navigational aid will not be built, despite the fact that it will be wanted by all concerned. The rational pursuit of private goals results in some of those goals not being realized. This is a problem which is referred to in the literature as the collective action problem.[8] In general, it arises when rational individuals desire collective consumption goals from which they cannot feasibly be excluded, and when each individual's contribution to the production process yields a *directly consequential* benefit which is less than the cost involved. Rational consumers will thus have strong incentives to take free rides on public goods.

Since pure public goods are something of an abstraction, rarely met in reality, it might be argued that the collective action problem can be solved by finding ways of excluding from consumption those who do not participate in producing the good. Exclusion is often a costly process, however, represents a public good to the group of existing contributors, and must be financed from somewhere. Furthermore, if excluding recalcitrants costs resources, it is quite possible that the benefits obtained (in terms of the increased likelihood of contributions) are less than the cost. This cost-benefit calculation will, of course, have an important strategic dimension. It may be worth excluding some free-riders at a loss, in order to prevent others from getting funny ideas about not paying. Whatever the results of these strategic calculations, it will be difficult under our core assumptions to provide mechanisms for excluding free-riders, precisely because such exclusion mechanisms are themselves public goods, subject to free-riding. Many goods may there-

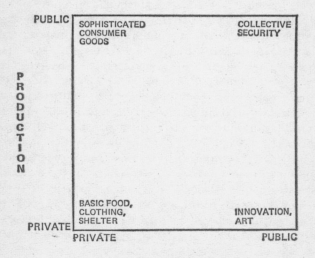

FIG. 1: THE PUBLICNESS OF GOALS

fore become effective collective consumption goods because of the problems of providing exclusion mechanisms.

The social context of goals is summarized in Figure 1. Goods can be either privately or jointly consumed, and either privately or jointly produced. Polar examples of each type of good include basic foodstuffs, which can be privately produced and consumed, and highly sophisticated consumer goods, which can be privately consumed, but require complex joint production. Collective security is jointly produced and must be jointly consumed. Finally, technical innovation or high art are often privately produced, but publicly consumed.

THE PROBLEM

The problem is the collective action problem, and relates to those goods which are both jointly produced and jointly consumed. While we assume that rational men will desire public goods, we do not need to assume that they will desire them intrinsically. At least one public good will be an instrumentally essential precursor to *private* goods-maximizing activity in any social environment. This public good is some system which leads to the honouring of agreements. Wherever there are gains from trade, rational individuals will want to make trading agreements with one another. The scope of these agreements will be drastically reduced if they are limited to those which must be consummated instantly. Transactions involving future commitments made by one or more parties can be affected only if those involved anticipate that the deal will be honoured (strictly, if the expectations associated with the deal being honoured exceed the investments involved). There must therefore be some chance that commitments will be honoured if any deals are to be made at all. A system which leads to the honouring of commitments would thus be a public good in itself, since the benefits would be available to all participants. Such a system would not be a pure public good, since it is possible to exclude people from its benefits. There is no doubt, however, that nearly all possible systems for ensuring that agreements are honoured exhibit high jointness of supply.

We have already seen that some form of collective security is another type of public good which will be instrumentally desired, even by the most pathologically individualistic utility-maximizer, since the necessity to invest private resources in weapons of offence and defence is essentially non-productive. (This is not to argue that such a being would actually participate in any collective agreements, but simply that they would perceive them to be beneficial.) Thus, there will be at least some jointly produced and jointly consumed goods which will be desired by rational individuals under our core assumptions. The remainder of the argument in this book will be mainly concerned with various potential solutions to the problem of how to produce these goods.

THE COLLECTIVE ACTION PROBLEM

We have just seen that a serious problem confronting rational individuals is that they may well desire public goods, yet be incapable of providing themselves with them. In the absence of any means of enforcing agreements, most people will assume that any marginal voluntary contribution they make towards the cost of producing a public good will greatly exceed any directly consequential marginal private gain. Thus, some mechanism for enforcing agreements is also a public good, since such a mechanism should facilitate the production of other public goods. Since it is a public good, it will tend not to be produced by individuals acting in a selfishly rational manner.

The difficulties faced by rational individuals who want to produce and consume public goods are usually referred to as the collective action problem. Specific statements of the collective action problem usually concern voluntary membership of particular political organizations, and voluntary contributions towards the cost of providing particular public goods, such as police forces and fire brigades. However, the problem in its most general form is a direct consequence of the situation outlined in the previous chapter. In all but the very smallest of groups (where the difference made by one contribution more or less might have a significant effect on the level of production), the interaction of rational individuals produces a situation in which each is worse off, as the public goods they desire are not produced.

In one circumstance, the collective action problem will solve itself. Those collective consumption goods requiring *pure* jointness of production will not be susceptible to free-riding by rational individuals. If production of a particular good requires the unanimous cooperation of the group, then the refusal of any single individual to participate in this production will result in the good not being produced. In those circumstances where the good is valued by each member of the group more than his contribution to the costs of production, it will not be rational for any to opt out. These goods will therefore be produced, despite the fact that they are collectively consumed. Examples of this type of good are rather hard to come by, but do exist. Each member of a group may, for example, be in possession of the same piece of secret information, and the preservation of this secret may be beneficial to them all. While each might, for personal reasons, like to tell the secret to people outside the group, provided that the secret is worth keeping, it will be kept. This is because secrets require pure jointness of production from the initiated. Once one person has refused to cooperate, the secret is no more. Each individual may destroy the secret single-handed, and because of this the secret, jointly produced and collectively consumed, will probably be produced. In general, since the collective action problem arises because each rational individual feels that any contribution towards the costs of the good exceeds the directly consequential marginal gain, it will not apply to goods requiring pure jointness of production, since this situation can never arise.

Olson himself suggests a number of other solutions. The first is to transform the public good in question into a private good (in our terms, to make it more private) by finding some way of excluding recalcitrants.[1] If this is possible, it will obviously do the trick, assuming that such exclusion costs nothing. A fire brigade could, for example, be organized in such a way as to protect the property only of those who contribute towards its upkeep. This form of fire protection would not be a purely private good, of course. If a particular group put out all its own fires efficiently, then the danger of fire spreading to damage the property of non-members would be reduced. Non-contributors would derive a worthwhile benefit from a fire service which costs them nothing. The members' fire brigade would be a private good with public externalities. The important point, however, is that the benefits coming to members as a *direct consequence of their contributions* are also worth paying for. Non-members get only some *general* lowering of local fire-risk (albeit for nothing), while members get fires put out in their own home (albeit at some cost). The partial exclusion of recalcitrants makes contribution much more attractive. There are many types of collective consumption good which it is technologically feasible to provide in this way. Private police forces can protect only subscribers, lighthouses can be transformed into radio beacons operating on secret frequencies, and so on. Some goods, however, cannot be physically produced in this manner. Examples include clean air or collective security. Alternative methods of provision must clearly be sought, if contributions cannot be enforced and recalcitrants cannot be excluded. Additionally, it may be very expensive to develop and produce goods from which non-contributors can be excluded, and such exclusion mechanisms therefore constitute a 'public bad'. (In other words, not having to provide them is a public good.) We have already seen that exclusion costs can render many goods effectively public. In short, for technical or economic reasons, many public goods cannot be feasibly 'privatized'.

The second method suggested by Olson is for groups to provide exclusive private benefits to members, in exchange for contributions towards the costs of producing public goods. These private benefits must be sufficiently cheap to produce, so that the surplus which is generated is large enough to provide the public good as well. It must be immediately noted that our assumptions do not permit organizations or groups of individuals to intrinsically value producing public goods *per se*. Hence we cannot automatically assume that, if a surplus is derived from the provision of private goods to members, a group will *therefore* devote this surplus to the provision of public goods. This assumption is, however, implicitly made by Olson. His example of a trade union, which sells insurance to its members in order to induce them to join, illustrates this problem. When it sells insurance, the trade union is an insurance broker engaged in private transactions. If these private transactions provide members with sufficient private surplus to justify their participation, they will participate whether or not a public good is provided by the union, since they are making a profit anyway. There is thus no reason to suppose that the public good will be provided. If the private transactions do *not* create a surplus for each individual, then the deficit they incur in dealing with the union will constitute a voluntary contribution towards the cost of providing the public goods. Since they cannot be forced to contribute, they will not do so, and we are back in the collective action problem. Unless we assume that there are some people who actually *want* to provide public goods from the profits of their private activities as a service to others, selling private goods on the side provides no solution. Such motivations do not form part of our description of rational man.

However, we have just seen that certain circumstances do exist in which private transactions can be arranged in such a way as to produce public goods as externalities. The members' fire brigade was one example; another is provided by a consumer research bureau which sells findings to subscribers on a private basis. Its research activities may contribute towards a general increase in the quality of the products under investigation. This will be a public good from which none can be excluded. The detailed findings are privately sold to subscribers, provided that the additional value of these exceeds the cost.[2] If sufficient consumers value the additional information, the research will be conducted, the private transactions concluded, and the public good produced as an externality. In this example, private transactions *actually produce* the public good as an externality; in Olson's example, private transactions *raise money* for the public good. The former requires no modification of our assumptions; the latter does.

Some public goods may therefore be produced even by utility maximizing individuals in a state of nature. There are public goods which can feasibly be produced privately, although once this happens they cease to be pure public goods.[3] In addition, there are public goods which can be realized as externalities to a set of private transactions. It is clear that there will be a considerable number of public goods which cannot be produced or consumed privately, and cannot be produced as externalities to private transactions. Indeed, nearly all common examples of public goods (such as collective security and clean air) fall into this category. We do not, therefore, have a solution to the 'real' collective action problem, which arises from the desire of rational individuals to consume non-excludable goods involving some, but not total, joint production. We move on to consider the first of our main alternatives.

LEVIATHAN

> The final cause, end, or design of men, who naturally love liberty, and dominion over others, in the introduction of that restraint upon themselves, in which we see them live in commonwealths, is the foresight of their own preservation, and of a more contented life thereby, that is to say, of getting themselves out from that miserable condition of war, which is necessarily consequent ... to the mutual passions of men, when there is no visible power to keep them in awe, and tie them by fear of punishment to the performance of their covenants ...[4]

Hobbes's argument about the ways in which public goods might be produced are well known and need not be extensively rehearsed. Most of the essential points are presented in Chapters XVII and XVIII of *Leviathan*.

To produce public goods, men must make covenants with one another, but 'covenants without the sword, are but words, and of no strength to secure a man at all.'[5]

> ... and therefore it is no wonder if there be somewhat else required, besides covenant, to make their agreement constant and lasting; which is a common power, to keep them in awe, and to direct their actions to the common benefit.
>
> The only way to erect such a common power ... is to confer all their power and strength upon one man, or upon one assembly of men, that may reduce all their wills ... unto one will ... and therein to submit their wills, every one to his will, and their judgements, to his judgement. This is more than consent, or concord; it is a real unity of them all ... made by covenant of every man with every man ... as if every man should say to every man, I *authorize and give up my right of governing myself, to this man, or to this assembly of men, on this condition, that thou give up thy right to him, and authorize all*

his actions in like manner. ... For by this authority, given him by every particular man in the commonwealth, he hath the use of so much power and strength conferred on him, that by terror thereof, he is enabled to perform the wills of them all, to peace at home, and mutual aid against their enemies abroad.[6]

Men move from a state of nature to a set of political arrangements which enable them to produce collective goods with one agreement, and one agreement only. They give the power to enforce all agreements (including the agreement in question) to one person. This person is a third party to the agreement, which can therefore involve him in no obligations.[7] Since his power to enforce agreements is unqualified, and since he is not a party to the agreement which gives him this power, at least one interpretation of Hobbes is that the leader who emerges is indeed a dictator. He cannot be removed from office, even if this becomes the unanimous wish of his subjects, since they have previously given him the power to enforce all agreements, including the agreement which gave him that power.

In the context of our definitions, one interpretation of Hobbes is as someone concerned to show at least one way in which public goods might eventually be produced, given his state-of-nature assumptions. The question which he cannot answer is why it would be *rational* (in the technical sense) for a group of men to give such unlimited power to anyone. It must first be stated quite clearly that a Hobbesian sovereign, in certain circumstances, can definitely provide one solution to the collective action problem. His activity enables men to make the covenants which are a necessary precondition for any such solution. Binding agreements are possible because they are enforced by a third party. If each member of a group desires some non-excludable good which can be efficiently produced and consumed only in concert, they can agree amongst themselves to do this in the confident expectation that each will fulfil his part of the bargain. Free-riders will be punished with a sanction which exceeds the benefits of opting out. Participation becomes rational because, once agreed upon, it costs more than it is worth to back out. It is individually rational for each member of the group to agree to the implementation of a mechanism for absolutely enforcing all binding agreements. Each can derive individual benefits from the public goods which can subsequently be produced.

The question is whether rational men will invest this power in one person who is under no obligation to them whatsoever. If the sovereign himself is rational, he will presumably exploit them without mercy. Once agreements become binding, of course, some public goods can be produced, whereas before there were none. Because the state of nature is such a dismal place, people might be better off even under a dictatorship. Faced only with the choice between a Hobbesian sovereign and a state of war, it might still be rational for each individual to choose the sovereign. The point, however, is that inhabitants of the state of nature might be able to do better than this. Can rational men devise a method of enforcing agreements which does not lay them open to this potential exploitation?

At this point, we must consider the precise impact on Hobbes's argument of some of his *social* assumptions. Critical here is the statement that 'man, whose joy consisteth in comparing himself with other men, can relish nothing but what is eminent.'[8] It is assumed that one of man's fundamental motivations causes him to be happy at others' material misfortune and sad at others' success. This imposes a serious constraint upon the possible political solutions to the state-of-nature problem, since it means that social life is essentially zero sum. What one man gains in eminence must be lost by another, since eminence is, by definition, relative.

The consequence of this emphasis on eminence-maximization is that no form of organization to enforce contracts will be stable, unless it is imposed from outside the system. This is because, even if an alternative method could be devised which raised everybody's utility income by facilitating the production of public goods, it would not be preferred by men concerned to maximize their eminence. Eminence-maximizing men may wish to implement a system which enables them to enforce agreements, but they can only agree to a system which is irreversible. Any *particular* agreement is bound to make some gain eminence and some lose it. A once-and-for-all system, therefore, is clearly the only stable one, since any other will quickly degenerate into a state of war. To the extent that eminence-maximizers desire public goods, they will prefer an imposed solution to a state of nature. Hobbes's move from a known state of nature to a commonwealth ruled by an absolute monarch is thus logical because he assumes that men are concerned to maximize eminence rather than utility.

We saw in the previous chapter that eminence-maximization is a socially determined goal, and therefore specifically excluded from our core assumptions. If a man is a utility-maximizer, however, he may well prefer to maintain arrangements which increase the provision of public goods. These arrangements may well be preferred, or at least not considered worse, by all members of a group of rational men. Thus, in principle, stable social arrangements which are not absolutely enforced may be devised to enable the provision of public goods by groups of rational men, provided that the free-rider problem can be overcome.

Rational man, however, must expect a Hobbesian sovereign to be rational. If the sovereign is rational, there is every reason to expect that he will be an extortionist, using the power vested in him to expropriate all he desires from his subjects. Rational man will also be aware of the mutual benefits to be derived from the provision of public goods, and will seek to achieve these in his own interest. The solutions he looks for can never involve an unconditional grant of power, however, unless the recipient is an other-worldly being who is essentially disinterested in any of the benefits to be derived from the natural environment. Since we have made no provision for such a creature in our assumptions, we must look for alternative arrangements.

To summarize the argument so far, Hobbesian man is lifted from his state of nature by an absolute monarch. This is the only alternative available to him if he is made unhappy by the success of others – a motivation which puts him in a zero-sum relationship with his fellows. No 'internal' arrangement can solve his collective action problem in a stable manner. This particular motivation is, however, ruled out by our own assumptions, whereby people are concerned with others only in an instrumental manner. Although a state of nature inhabited by self-obsessed utility-maximizers might look rather similar to one inhabited by Hobbesian man, the methods available for solving the collective action problem will be quite different. Unlike Hobbesian man, self-obsessed utility-maximizers might *all* be satisfied with some stable arrangement which facilitates the provision of public goods without granting absolute power to any one individual. There is therefore every reason to suppose that they will seek to achieve such an arrangement.

ANARCHY

Perhaps the most obvious alternative to granting a monopoly of power to one individual is to grant it to none, a solution which we will describe as 'anarchistic'. One way of doing this is to establish a system of enforcing agreements upon which every member of the group can have an important impact. Mutually beneficial agreements between rational individuals, including agreements to produce public goods, stand little chance of success if any party to them suspects that others will not fulfil their side of the bargain. 'Anarchistic' agreements are not enforced by any outside agency, but are constructed in such a way that they still contain incentives for all parties to honour their commitments, including commitments which will be consummated at some time in the future.

Michael Taylor discusses this type of solution to the collective action problem in *Anarchy and Cooperation*.[9] He argues that, if agreements of this sort facilitate the provision of public goods, they undermine one of the most pervasive and persuasive liberal justifications for the role of the state. Taylor presents the collective action problem as a Prisoners' Dilemma supergame, and illustrates the game strategies which combine to produce stable and cooperative outcomes without recourse to any external authority.

THE PRISONERS' DILEMMA AND PUBLIC GOODS

The Prisoners' Dilemma is a traditional preoccupation of rational choice theorists. The original allegory concerns two known criminals who are caught red-handed while committing some minor offence, such as stealing a car. The police know, but cannot prove, that they were involved in a much more serious crime, an armed bank robbery. The criminals are separated, and each is offered the following deal: 'If you give evidence against your accomplice, and he is convicted of the armed robbery, you will walk out of here a free man. If you don't, then you will go to jail for stealing the car anyway, and quite possibly take the whole blame for the bank job.' Both captives are old lags, and know the score. They know that, if neither gives evidence, they will both get one year for car theft. They know that, if one keeps quiet and the other gives evidence, the one carrying the whole blame for the bank job gets ten years. Finally, each knows that, if both give evidence, both will be convicted of armed robbery, getting maybe a two-year reduction in sentence for helping the police. These pay-offs, denominated in years in jail and therefore negative, are summarized in Figure 2.

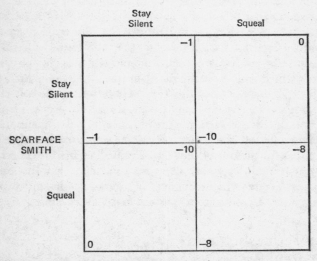

FIG. 2: PAY-OFFS FOR THE PRISONERS' DILEMMA

The pay-off in the top right-hand corner of each box goes to Jones, and that in the bottom left to Smith.

There are four possible outcomes. These are mutual silence, mutual squealing and either Smith or Jones squealing while the other stays silent. We can quickly see that, if they play this game only once, both Smith and Jones must squeal. This is because, *whatever* the other does, each does best by squealing. If Scarface stays silent, then Wildman does best by squealing, getting no years in jail rather than one. If Scarface squeals, then Wildman does best by squealing, getting eight years in jail, rather than ten. Both squeal, since both face exactly the same 'dilemma'. The consequence is that both do time for the robbery, despite the fact that both would be better off staying silent and simply doing their time for the car theft. The pursuit of individual rationality inevitably leads to an outcome which is deplored by both criminals.

In general terms, the Prisoners' Dilemma is any game in which the pay-offs for each player are arranged in the order of those in Figure 2. General discussions of the game usually describe the two strategies available to each player as defection (rather than squealing) and cooperation (rather than staying silent). It is always the case in a one-off game that individually rational self-interest produces an outcome (mutual defection) which is regarded by all as inferior to an alternative outcome (mutual cooperation), which could be achieved if each behaved differently. All choose to defect, however, because defection is the dominant strategy for each. Each is better off defecting if the others cooperate, and better off defecting if the others defect.

This is not at all modified by allowing the players to talk to each other, as long as agreements between them cannot be enforced. If they agree to mutual cooperation, each nevertheless has both the willingness and the ability to defect from this agreement. Each will expect the other to do likewise, and is therefore left with no alternative but to defect. The two players in the Prisoners' Dilemma face a collective action problem. Both would prefer the outcome to be mutual cooperation rather than mutual damaging. They *can* combine in a joint effort to bring this about. Yet, each individually cannot make the situation worse by defecting, although individual and collective welfare deteriorates considerably if they both think like this. Mutual cooperation, as opposed to mutual damaging, is a public good which can be produced only if both sides cooperate. Although both sides would prefer to cooperate, even sophisticated rational behaviour can only result in failure.

The players can get around this problem, and produce public goods, if some means can be found of leading them to expect that any agreement that they might make will be adhered to. If someone 'outside' the game punishes players every time that they fail to keep their word, for example, a binding agreement between them is made possible. Cooperation therefore becomes far more probable. The 'outside' authority in this case fulfils a role closely analogous to that of the Hobbesian sovereign, or, for example, an organized crime syndicate in the original example. The syndicate, by arranging concrete overcoats for those who break deals made with its members, would make these deals much more binding and, therefore, much more likely to materialize. If the players are *forced* into this situation, they may derive some benefits from it, but we have just seen that they would never voluntarily submit themselves to such a system. The power vested in the outside authority could be used to exploit them, unless that authority is assumed to be entirely benevolent.

If the Prisoners' Dilemma is repeated over and over again by the same players, and if, at any point in the sequence, all previous moves are known to each player, then they are playing what is known as a supergame. Taylor shows that Prisoners' Dilemma supergames can, in certain circumstances, result in mutually cooperative outcomes without recourse to an outside agency which enforces agreements. If this is the case, then the collective action problems which these games represent can be similarly 'solved'.

CONDITIONAL COOPERATION

When a *sequence* of games is played, new strategies emerge which are 'conditional'. One player can say to another, for example, 'I'll start off by cooperating. Thereafter, I'll do whatever you did in the previous game. If you cooperated, I'll cooperate; if you damaged me, I'll damage you.' Such strategies, explored extensively in *Anarchy and Cooperation*, do produce rational mutual cooperation in certain circumstances. This is because each player is now made worse off *as a direct result of choosing a damaging strategy*. Disrupting the conditional cooperation by defecting yields a short-term benefit for the single game in which the defection takes place. However, because of the nature of the agreement, such a defection ensures that mutual damaging will take place in the subsequent games. Since both players prefer mutual cooperation to mutual damaging, the defector loses in the long run. The one-off benefits of defection are eroded by the losses resulting from the continuous mutual damaging which this defection directly produces.

Consider the example of two rational individuals deciding whether to spend resources on arming themselves. Once armed, each will have to expend further resources maintaining these weapons in lethal condition. They can each decide that neither will start arming unless the other does. Each will be adopting the conditional strategy, 'I'll cooperate with you as long as you cooperate with me. Once you stop cooperating, we will both be worse off, because I will stop cooperating too.' Each will therefore know that, despite the quick profit which might be made out of a surprise attack on an unarmed opponent, the long-term disadvantages produced by this make such an attack unattractive. These long-term disadvantages arise from the fact that, once conditional cooperation is upset, both sides (including the attacker) will have to continue to spend money on weapons of offence and defence, while the net result will be that they are just as evenly matched as they were when they started. The profits from the surprise attack would quickly disappear.

In the two-person game, mutual cooperation is a public good for the players; but a more general statement of aspects of the collective action problem is provided by the n-person Prisoners' Dilemma. Consider, for example, a group of people, each of whom was trying to decide whether to invest resources in nasty weapons. Obviously, each would most like to be the only armed member of the group, and would least like to be unarmed in a group where at least one of the others was armed. If none are armed, or if all are armed, there is a stand-off. Clearly an unarmed stand-off is preferable to an armed stand-off, since it is cheaper. In this example, one individual can bring about everyone else's least preferred outcome, simply by becoming armed.

It should once more be clear that conditional cooperation may solve the problem. If the decision to arm were taken once and once only, then mutual damaging would be the inevitable result, since each player is better off becoming armed, whatever the others decide to do. If the decision is taken continuously, however, because being armed involves continuous expenditure, then each of the players can decide to cooperate as long as they all cooperate, in just the same way as they did in the two-person example. Conditional cooperation will be stable for just the same reasons. While each player might make a profit by defecting in the short term, this course of action will not be attractive, because it directly produces the mutual damaging which makes everyone, including the defector, worse off. This is because there is no point in *anyone* cooperating if *everyone* is not cooperating. Since each knows that his action, and his action alone, destroys cooperation in subsequent games, individual rationality may now dictate cooperation.

Taylor argues that such conditional cooperation between the players is likely to provide stable solutions to the problem if these conditions are met. Firstly, the group must be relatively small, since the probability of 'wildcat' defections will increase as the group gets larger. Secondly, the group must be small enough, or be so organized, for individual defection to be monitored. Thirdly, the benefits of defection, determined by the specific pay-off of the game in question, must be small relative to the benefits of future cooperation. Since some may discount future utility relative to present utility, while others may value future utility more than present utility, these 'discount functions' must be taken into account when future benefits are assessed. Those who discount future utility may be tempted to defect if the immediate benefits they can derive from defection exceed the future (discounted) benefits of cooperation. The more 'future-oriented' members of the group there are – and the less they discount their future utility – the greater the chance that they will adhere to a conditional agreement of the type under consideration.

If the group is not too large, and if the group members do not discount future utility too heavily, there are potential equilibrium solutions to Prisoners' Dilemma supergames which yield cooperation, yet do not require external enforcement. These are Taylor's anarchistic arrangements, which may lead to some public goods being produced, even by groups of self-obsessed utility-maximizers. The particular goods which can be produced under such arrangements will largely be a matter for empirical study, as will the specific nature of the discount functions of the individual members. Some public goods, however, cannot be produced under these arrangements, because they require larger-scale production than an anarchic group can support, because the benefits of opting out are too great (compared to the discounted future benefits of opting in) or because opting out might be difficult to detect.

The examples of *n*-person Prisoners' Dilemmas that we have so far considered represent special cases, where the defection of a *single* individual renders everyone else worse off than they would be if *everyone* defected. In these cases the argument, as we have seen, is relatively straightforward. This particular condition will obtain, however, only in a very small minority of cases. It will much more frequently be the case that the defection of any particular individual from the mutually cooperative solution leaves everyone else worse off than they were before that defection, but *still better off* than they would be if everyone defected. We have not yet demonstrated that the mutually cooperative outcome is stable in those situations where the remainder of the group would find it rational to continue cooperating to produce the public good after one or more members have defected. In the terminology of the previous chapter, the solutions advanced so far apply only to those goods exhibiting pure jointness of production. The problem we are left with is to explain the provision of goods which exhibit jointness of supply and some, but not total, jointness of production. This problem arises, of course, because potential defectors will know that cooperation will remain rational for the rest of the group after they have defected. Knowing this, it is reasonable to suppose that the good will still be produced, and knowing *this*, defection and free-riding become rational once more, even in the supergame. Every rational member of the group will think this and defect, and production of the good will collapse. It is not hard to see that this is the 'real' collective action problem. The case of public goods exhibiting pure jointness of production is, as we have seen, an example of a type of public good which is not susceptible to free-riding, because the defection of each individual has directly consequential and privately damaging results. Taylor acknowledges this problem, and allows for free-riding on goods which, while jointly supplied, are not *purely* jointly produced. He argues that, in those cases where one defection does not make the rest of the group worse off than they would be if all defected, then that defection will take place and the rest will continue to cooperate. By this process, the group will shed cooperators, until a point is reached when any further defection would render continued cooperation by the rest counter-productive. At that point, claims Taylor, stable cooperation will ensue.[10] The residual group of cooperators will still be better off than they would be if all defected. If any one of them now defects, however, they will all be better off giving up their cooperative strategies, and defecting themselves. Thus, none finds it worthwhile opting for the short-term benefits of defection. In effect, Taylor argues that the group will shrink until it reaches the point at which unanimous cooperation is necessary for the continued production of the public good. This is the point at which the good exhibits pure jointness of production with respect to the residual producing group. Of course, it will be jointly *supplied* to the group as a whole, including the free-riders.

The first problem with this interpretation is that it rests upon an assumption that the process of defection is extremely orderly. The players are assumed to defect one at a time, until a point is reached when further defections render continued cooperation unprofitable. Analytically, this assumption does the trick, but there is an important reason why it is very unrealistic. It is clear that everyone would rather be outside the residual group of cooperators than inside it. Those on the outside will be able to consume the jointly supplied good without contributing to the cost of its production. Every rational member of the group will realize this, and want to be in this position. It thus seems likely that there will be a mad scramble. Everyone will want to defect early on, in order to avoid being placed in the position where their continued cooperation is essential to the further provision of the good. While everyone knows that *someone* must be left with their finger in the dyke, no one wants it to be them. During this scramble, it is quite possible that the group size will plummet through the critical level. In short, as soon as everyone realizes that some defections can be tolerated, everyone will want to be one of the tolerated defectors. This is more likely to produce a stampede than an orderly process of defection, and the possibility of such stampedes makes less likely the provision of public goods on the basis of a critical group size.

A second problem with this solution is that it rests on a very sweeping assumption about the symmetry of the pay-offs to each player. Taylor makes this assumption, and claims in a note that it is not critical.[11] However, if every player does not receive an identical pay-off in identical situations, then it is quite possible that there is no *particular* size of residual group which yields stable cooperation. If, at any point, different members of the residual group value the good which they are producing differently, there will be no one point in the game when they all simultaneously realize that any further defections render further cooperation counter-productive. Those who value the good less than the others will decide that further cooperation is irrational before those who value the good more. There will be a point at which the group is still too large for those who value the good highly (they value the good enough to tolerate further defection), but at the same time too small for those who value the good less (who do not value the good enough to tolerate even the present level of defections). Thus, if the pay-offs are not symmetrical, it is almost certain that the group will have no 'critical mass'. This critical mass is crucial to Taylor's equilibrium solution in all cases except that of pure jointness of production, where unanimous cooperation is required if the good is to be produced at all.

Another sweeping assumption which is necessary before a stable residual group of cooperators emerges is that they all discount their future utility income by exactly the same amount. If the members of the residual group have different discount rates for their future utility, then they will arrive at the decision to defect at different points in the process. The consequence, once more, will be that the group will have no unique 'critical mass'. Those who discount their future utility rather heavily will defect before those who hardly discount it at all. A situation could easily arise where some members of the residual group of cooperators were defecting because the group was still too large (they are prepared to consider the benefits of cooperation stretching far into the future), while other members of the group were defecting because it was already too small (they are not prepared to wait long for the benefits of cooperation).

Even if there is orderly defection, absolute symmetry of pay-offs and identical discount functions for the cooperators, there is the problem that this solution does no more than guarantee some very minimal level of production of the good in question. Some public goods will have 'all-or-nothing' production functions, so that you either have them or you don't, with no halfway house. Most, however, will be capable of being produced at a number of different levels, if not at a continuously varying level. In these cases, the level of production which will actually be achieved by the conditional cooperation of the residual group will be the bare minimum which it can profitably sustain, assuming that the level of production is in some way proportional to the size of the producing group. Any level of production above this bare minimum will produce defections, until the minimum point is reached and further defections would yield a loss. (It is interesting that Taylor's examples all tend to come from the 'all-or-nothing' class of public goods where this qualification does not apply.)

In conclusion then, Taylor's solution applies firstly when unanimous cooperation is necessary to produce the goods. In these circumstances, it might be argued that there is no collective action problem. If pure joint production is not required, the solution will produce bare minimum levels of the public good if, and only if, the following conditions are met. Firstly, any defections prior to the attainment of the residual group of producers must be sufficiently orderly that the precise critical group size can in fact be achieved (despite the pressures towards chaotic defection). Secondly, pay-offs to all participants must be completely symmetrical. Thirdly, all participants must have identical discount functions. These conclusions can best be illustrated by an example.

The 'state of nature' example used early on by Taylor is the 'tragedy of the commons'.[12] A group of herdsmen each have access to a piece of common pasture. Each has a private incentive to graze as many animals on the land as possible, yet the pasture can only support so many animals. There will come a point when the addition of another animal to the commons will reduce the yield of all animals who live there, because of overgrazing. Despite this, the herdsmen will continue adding animals to their stock, because a single animal added by a single herdsman still yields a private surplus. The herdsman takes any benefit arising from the extra animal, while any consequent losses will be shared by all the others. All will therefore go on adding to their stock. The result of this is that they will all be worse off as the commons deteriorate, becoming overgrazed and possibly even suffering ecological collapse. The commons, a public good for the herdsmen, may be destroyed, because users face a collective action problem.

The public good in this case can be measured more precisely as the yield per animal which the commons can sustain. This good exhibits pure jointness of supply: the yield is identical for each herdsman. Up to the point at which the yield starts to decline with the addition of further animals, the good also exhibits no jointness of production: no cooperation is required for optimum output. Once this point has been passed, the good exhibits jointness of production, since the action of any herdsman in adding to stock reduces the yield per animal. Taylor's 'solution' to the problem facing the herdsmen would be for each to conditionally limit the size of his stock to a level consistent with the highest possible yield. If one of them defects from this agreement and adds to the size of his stock, the yield goes down, but the conditional cooperation of the others is still rational; they still do better by continuing to limit the size of their own stock, rather than competing with each other to get as much as possible on to the commons. Others will defect and add to their stock, until a point is reached when the residual group is so small that, if any more defect, continued cooperation will no longer be worthwhile. This will be because the residual group would not be large enough to influence the level of overgrazing of the commons, to the extent that each member is better off than he would be in joining the scramble to graze more stock. When this point is reached, the group will not lose any more members, and some form of stable cooperation will be achieved.

Firstly, we can see straight away from this example that this agreement will yield considerably sub-optimal quantities of the public good in question. Indeed, it is part of the essence of the solution that members of the group of cooperators will defect until cooperation is barely worthwhile (the point at which, if it was worth any less, it would not be worthwhile). Secondly, we see that the assumption of symmetry demands that each member of the residual group has a herd of precisely the same size. If this is not the case, then those with a larger herd will be prepared to go on cooperating for longer than those with a small herd, since the total benefits of a given level of control are greater for the former than the latter. Thus, the small herdsman will defect before the large herdsman, and there will be no single critical size for the group of herdsmen as a whole. For the small herdsmen, the benefits of adding to their existing stock will more quickly outweigh the loss of yield ensuing if cooperation were to collapse. Thirdly, we can see that those who discount their benefits rather steeply, for example old herdsmen, will defect before those who consider benefits stretching a long way into the future, for example young herdsmen. The benefits of long-term cooperation would seem greater to the latter than to the former. Cooperation would stop seeming worthwhile to the old men at an earlier point than it would for the young men.

This example also shows that *some* form of cooperation would emerge at *some* point, just before ecological disaster. When the addition of one animal would tip the scales towards eco-catastrophe, then even the person who added that animal would be worse off as a direct consequence of this action, and would therefore refrain. If stability is to be reached before this point, then the herdsmen must have identically sized herds and an identical attitude to future utility income. If these restrictive conditions are met, and if they do not panic in an attempt to get out of the group of cooperators before they are 'trapped' in it, then stable cooperation may result as the commons are on the brink of ecological disaster.

The tragedy of the commons illustrates the different problems produced by different types of public good. When the commons is on the point of collapse, it becomes an 'all-or-nothing' good. At this point it is also a good requiring *pure* jointness of production, since the action of any individual can destroy the whole thing. As we saw earlier, the collective action problem does not really arise in these circumstances, since non-cooperative behaviour by individuals makes each directly worse off. Before this point is reached, however, when the good is measured in terms of yield per animal, the good is not of the all-or-nothing variety, and has a continuous production function. If an individual chooses not to cooperate, this action does not *necessarily* make him worse off, although it does make everyone else worse off. In these circumstances, the conditionally cooperative solution might be stable, but only at a level which is barely profitable for those concerned, and then only under highly restrictive assumptions.

We have already seen that 'all-or-nothing' goods are more susceptible to anarchist production than goods with continuous production functions. There is a further property of public goods which renders them more or less susceptible to these arrangements. A particular public good may be such that, in order for it to be produced at all, it is necessary to *commit* a future flow of resources. Most goods involving large-scale capital investment are like this. Such commitments of future resources would never be achieved by the conditional agreements which underpin anarchistic solutions. If a commitment is undertaken by the group, the free-rider problem reappears at once. A potential defector would know that the group was bound to provide resources for the collective good concerned, whether or not he contributes. The only way of indulging in large-scale public capital expenditure would be for each individual to save up his total contribution in advance, and for everyone to contribute all at once. This might work if all the conditions specified above were satisfied, but even if this was the case, there would be considerable delay in producing the good. This would be a public bad. It is thus even less likely that collective goods involving capital investment could be produced under anarchistic arrangements than it is that other goods could be.

THREATS AND COOPERATION

So far, the conclusions have been largely negative. The fact that it is just about possible to produce sub-optimal amounts of certain restricted categories of public goods would hardly, in itself, undermine many arguments justifying the existence of the state. This problem has arisen, in part, because one course of action open to the participants has been ignored. This is to *threaten* potential free-riders with dire consequences if they pursue the course of action which rational self-interest would otherwise indicate.

We will consider only threats which can be enacted within the context of the game, since, if a threat to carry out some punishment completely irrelevant to the game can be enacted, this amounts to no more than the imposition of a particular outcome by the stronger party. We will return to this type of punishment in a later section. Threats *can* often be made within the confines of a particular game, however. A group of cooperators can threaten to cease production of the public good if anyone defects from their ranks, *even if* rational calculation would otherwise indicate continued production. The group would in fact come to the conditional agreement, 'If anyone defects, we all defect, whether or not that might appear to be rational.' This does not guarantee that defection will not take place, but sets up quite a complex strategic interaction between the potential defector and the rest of the group. If the group expected to make only this one agreement, there would be no problem; defectors would simply ignore the threat if continued cooperation was rational for the rest of the group after their departure. If the group has made, or expects to make, other such agreements, things are different; it may now be rational for them to punish defectors by terminating their agreement to cooperate, even when it is still profitable. The reason for doing this would be so that potential defectors from the other agreements made by the group would know that it meant business. The group need sustain no overall loss if winding up a profitable agreement reduced the risk of defection from any other agreement it had made. Winding up the agreement would yield an instrumental pay-off in terms of increased credibility. Once potential defectors knew that group credibility was at stake, they would be less likely to defect. It is thus possible that stable cooperation would ensue, since defection would lead to directly consequential losses to the defector, provided that he valued the good in question more than his contribution towards the costs of providing it. This tendency towards stable cooperation is brought about by consideration of the array of Prisoners' Dilemma games that any given group is likely to be playing simultaneously.

Consider, for example, a 'tragedy of *several* commons'. In addition to the common land on which the herdsmen graze their livestock, there is the common pond from which they fish, which is susceptible to over-fishing, the common wood in which they hunt their game which is susceptible to over-hunting, and the common air which they breathe, which is susceptible to pollution from their fires. If nothing is done about it, the rational behaviour of the herdsmen will lead to the collapse of each of these vital aspects of their livelihood. They can avoid this by limiting their behaviour in each case with a series of separate agreements, each of which takes the form: 'We will each limit our grazing (hunting, fishing, fires) as long as everyone else does. As soon as anyone breaks this agreement, it is null and void.' If a hunter was thinking of breaking the hunting agreement, he might well be deterred by the knowledge that the group would have to punish him (as well as themselves) by tearing up the hunting agreement. This would be because they could not countenance the possibility that others would be tempted to break other agreements made by the group, if they did not demonstrate that they meant what they said. Considering the hunting agreement in isolation, it might well be rational to continue to cooperate over hunting in face of a defecting hunter, because continuing cooperation still yielded a net surplus for the remaining cooperators. However, this surplus could be wiped out by defections from other agreements made by the group. The group would punish the defecting hunter, because it could not risk the possibility that failure to do so would encourage defecting fishermen, herdsmen or fire-burners. The collapse of hunting which might well ensue could be a price which members of the group were prepared to pay to safeguard the future of their grazing-land, their fish-pond and the air they breathed. Knowing this to be the case makes the hunters less likely to defect. Such agreements are anarchistic in the sense that they are entirely 'self-policing' and do not rely upon any external enforcement. It is quite possible that they will be stable for any size of group above the minimum level necessary for profitable cooperation. There is thus no reason to suppose that the level of production of the goods involved will be necessarily sub-optimal.

ANARCHY AND NORMS

We have seen above that 'anarchistic' solutions to collective action problems seem more appropriate when the goods concerned involve the modification of behaviour than when they involve the investment of tangible resources. Goods involving the modification of behaviour can be thought of as 'norms', and we might pause to consider whether Taylor's view of anarchy does provide a theory of norms. This is particularly important in view of the conclusion that one particular collective consumption good greatly expedites the provision of other collective consumption goods. This is a system which leads to the honouring of agreements. This good would be anarchistically produced if everyone voluntarily adhered to a norm of honesty. Some recent accounts of norms have indeed concentrated on the Prisoners' Dilemma game. We have seen that, 'if nothing is done about it', the Prisoners' Dilemma can result in outcomes which are deplored by all concerned. Is using a system of norms one of the things which might be done about it? I will take as the starting point of this discussion the recent argument advanced by Edna Ullmann-Margalit in *The Emergence of Norms.*[13]

Ullmann-Margalit claims that social interactions with the structure of the Prisoners' Dilemma 'are prone to generate' norms.[14] I will argue that, although the observation of cooperative norms would resolve the problems created by the Prisoners' Dilemma to everyone's benefit, such observation generates second-order collective action problems, which must themselves be resolved if norms are to be effective.

On the basis of our core assumptions, we must remember that rational men are motivated by more than the desire to conform, or to be liked, when they bow to the 'significant social pressure' which

Ullmann-Margalit suggests leads them to observe norms of obligation.[15] Indeed, we must insist that rational men do not bow to
significant social pressure as a result of any *intrinsic* desire to do so,
but as an instrumental means of furthering their individual self-
interest. To do otherwise would be to assume a socially defined
motivation which was irreducible to purely individualistic motivations, and thus to abandon the search for fundamental potential
explanations of social norms. In other words, if we allow people to
bow to social pressure 'because they want to,' we might as well
allow them to cooperate with one another for the same reason.
Thus, rational men observe norms because defection is punished.
This position is not denied in *The Emergence of Norms*, where
Ullmann-Margalit argues that 'what is required is a reduction in
the pay-offs (of defection) to at least the level of the pay-offs (of
cooperation), but preferably to a considerably lower level than
that'.[16]

Thus, norms of obligation, by associating sanctions with the
choice of uncooperative strategies, render such strategies unattractive, and consequently everyone is better off. The sanctions
which underpin norms are not just any old sanctions; they are
collectively determined and enacted. If soldiers who desert their
battle lines are liable to be caught and executed, then the temp-
tation to desert is greatly reduced. A rational soldier will now
desert only if the probability of being killed by the enemy exceeds
the probability of being caught and executed by his own side. Staying at the front in these circumstances does not, however, look
much like adhering to a norm. It looks much more like responding
to coercion. If the threat of execution did not exist, then a norm of
'honourable behaviour under fire' might resolve the Deserters' Dilemma, but only if deviation from this norm involved costs. Ruling
out the possibility of intrinsic private desires to conform to social
norms, these costs must manifest themselves as losses of utility in
other spheres of activity. Perhaps the deserter's colleagues will
refuse to deal with him in the future and effectively exclude him
from their group. The deserter is not worse off because he is excluded from a group to which he intrinsically wants to belong, but
because belonging to the group enables him to realize gains from

joint production, trade and so on. Adhering to a group norm for fear of being excluded from the group looks more like our conventional understanding of norm-oriented behaviour.

The problem is not, however, to explain why people conform to norms, but why people punish deviants. For the reasons discussed above, we cannot hand this task to an 'outside' authority. Norms, therefore, must be enforced collectively. They do not *in themselves* solve the collective action problems broadly represented by the Prisoners' Dilemma, but rather push this problem one stage further back along the analytical chain, generating new collective action problems, which are susceptible (or not, as the case may be) to conventional solutions.

The collective enactment of social punishment has been discussed, as the 'Punishment Dilemma', by James Buchanon in *The Limits of Liberty*.[17] When a group of rational individuals must police themselves with respect to certain areas of behaviour (and this is essentially the role of norms of obligation), then the costs of punishment must be paid by members of the group. These will only be met by private individuals when the private benefits of administering punishment exceed the private costs. In these circumstances, there will be no need for norms anyway. If private deviation provokes private enforcement, then the social pressure which underpins norms of obligation becomes redundant. Norms only become necessary when it is the collective, as opposed to the private, interest of group members to restrain recalcitrance. Thus, if the enforcement of norms is costly, these costs must be collectively borne. This aspect of the Punishment Dilemma is that, while the *threat* of punishment might deter potential recalcitrants, the costly *enactment* of punishment generates another collective action problem.[18] If potential recalcitrants judge that this second-order collective action problem cannot be resolved, then the threat of punishment will lose its deterrent effect.

If, on the other hand, punishment costs nothing, there is no reason to conclude, given our assumptions, that it will be conditional upon any particular transgression. Consider, for example, the possibility of excluding a recalcitrant from the group. Either that individual contributes something to the group or not. If he or she does contribute something, then exclusion has costs, and the previous argument applies. If he or she contributes nothing, and can be excluded without cost, then they will be excluded anyway, whether or not they adhere to group norms. In general, if sanctions involve no costs and can realize benefits, then they will be applied regardless of the behaviour of the recipient.

Instead of punishing those who deviate, the group may reward those who conform with some good which it can collectively produce at little or no cost. Examples of this type of good include honour, prestige, status and so on. (Honour is the one solution advanced by Ullmann-Margalit which does not ultimately depend on coercion.)[19] Some rewards can of course be produced very cheaply by a group, involving at most the construction of attractive badges for the recipients to pin to their chests. These may then be exchanged for rigorous observance of social norms of obligation by private individuals. Two points need to be made. In the first place, the constraints of our methodology require us to assume that such rewards are valued only for instrumental reasons. To do otherwise would be to impute *a priori* a social motivation to explain a social process. In the second place, such rewards are presumably instrumentally valued because they increase the *relative* ability of the recipient to realize intrinsically valued goals. Since honour and the like are not intrinsically productive, their instrumental value must lie in the benefits which can be derived from a superior social position. For this reason, they must be in short supply, since it is not possible for everyone in the group to improve their relative social position. Since these goods will be in short supply, individuals will compete for them, bidding up the price until an equilibrium is reached. In this case, 'the price' will be denominated in terms of the sacrifices involved in the observance of norms by rational individuals, when they could otherwise realize a surplus by defecting.

This appears to be a cheap and satisfactory solution to the problem. Although everyone who observes norms cannot be rewarded with enhanced social status (there is not enough of it to go around), if this status has sufficient instrumental value, people might compete with each other over the private sacrifices they are prepared to make in the hope of being socially rewarded. Plausible as this might seem, there is one problem. Social rewards will be valued if they help the owner to realize other goals which are individualistic and asocial in character. To the extent that these other goals are in short supply, those who do not receive honour and status will be worse off. Thus, while honour and status in themselves are cheap, if not free, the consequences of honour and status will be expensive for the rest of the group. These costs must be collectively borne by the rest, and their allocation will thus present the group with a collective action problem. Furthermore, because honour and status are essentially in short supply, and because they are collectively produced, collective decisions will have to be taken on the identity of the recipients, and these collective decisions may themselves involve costs. Producing social rewards has effective costs, particularly for those who do not receive them. The allocation of these costs creates a collective action problem. The Rewarders' Dilemma is, of course, really the other side of the Punishment Dilemma. In each case, the benefits of increased adherence to norms are public goods which are more or less costly to produce. In each case, we still need to understand the basis on which these costs are raised.

We have seen that, although the observance of norms might help to resolve the collective action problems represented by the Prisoners' Dilemma, the enactment of the rewards and punishments which encourage norm-observance generates second-order collective action problems. Thus, norms do not *in themselves* resolve particular collective action problems; rather, they transform one type of collective action problem into another. The role of norms in this context is explicable only if the new collective action problems they generate are more easily resolved than the original collective action problems which generated them.

Norm-observance will be a public good for a group to the extent that the benefits are available to all, but do not depend upon the behaviour of any particular individual. I may benefit when the rest of my colleagues observe norms, whether or not I myself observe them. If, in a battle, there is no chance of deserting soldiers being identified and shot, if all that is stopping fellow-soldiers from deserting is their adherence to a norm of honour, and if my personal contribution to the course of the battle is negligible, then my rational course of action is 'dishonourable' desertion. Only if my fellow-soldiers can collectively implement the rewards and/or punishments which underpin the norm of honour, am I likely to stay at my post. Otherwise, I will take a free ride to home and safety. Honour resolves the Deserters' Dilemma only if the collective action upon which its effect depends is likely to take place.

The case that the second-order collective action problems generated by norms are more easily resolvable than the collective action which generate the norms in question, rests upon assumptions about the precise nature of the rewards and punishments involved. We have seen that these rewards and punishments are socially generated, and include the exclusion of the group or the award of social status and prestige by the group to those who conform. If I am rational, therefore, I will try to avoid my contributions towards the costs of their provision, since I can enjoy the benefits regardless. These goods do have a particular property, however, which makes them less susceptible to free-riding than other collective consumption goods. They require the unanimous, or near-unanimous, cooperation of the whole group if they are to be produced at all; in other words, they require jointness of production, since they can be destroyed by the action of any single member of the group. These goods being 'immune' from the collective action problem, then, if valued by every member of the group, they will be produced. No individual has any incentive to take a free ride, since it makes him directly worse off by destroying the valued rewards and punishments which underpin norms of obligation may thus be much less susceptible to the collective action problem than the goods which those norms help to produce. It may plausibly be argued that both the exclusion of recalcitrants from the group, and the award of social status, are goods which possess this property.

It is clear, for instance, that the exclusion of a recalcitrant from transactions with the group can be effected only if all members of the group refuse to deal with the excluded individual. If someone in

Shirley Leishman Books Ltd.
83 Uwkalfe St.
235-7486

0 2 - 0 9 - 8 3

03   0.49
03   0.49
03   0.49
2 A   1.47 T
      5.00 CATO
      3.53 CG

00000 № 3613

the group will deal with outsiders, then they may profitably act as their agent in transactions with other group members. If you refuse to sell me goods I want because I am a coward or a liar, then the sanction has no effect if my friend, who has not been excluded, may purchase these goods on my behalf. The only way to enact this sanction will be to exclude my friend too, so that the remaining members of the group are unanimously refusing to deal with me. Exclusion, therefore, involves the unanimous cooperation of group members.

Similarly, the award of social status will be instrumentally valued only if it is recognized by a vast majority of the group. The instrumental value of this status arises from the consequent ability of the holder to increase utility income. The status *in itself* is not a valuable tool in the same sense as a combine harvester or a shotgun. It amounts to a statement by the group that the holder is less likely than others to be challenged if he or she desires certain goods. This has the effect of reducing the holder's competition costs or, for the same expenditure, increasing appropriations of goods. If status is not unanimously recognized, then it becomes much less valuable, since the holder will still have to compete for those goods to which he or she is supposedly entitled. Status does not require unanimous agreement, but it is made much more valuable by such agreement.

The rewards and punishments associated with norms of obligation may require the almost unanimous cooperation or agreement of the group. They are thus destroyed by defection, and are more likely to avoid the production problems which beset other types of collective good.

To summarize, this interpretation of the role of norms of obligation runs as follows. Norms, if they are observed, may 'anarchistically' resolve a whole series of collective action problems. Norms will be observed only if they are underpinned by socially generated but instrumentally valued rewards and punishments. Considering the set of norms as a whole, these punishments may take the form of excluding recalcitrants from the group, while the rewards involve the award of social prestige or status. The problem of collectively enforcing adherence to a set of norms, and hence of solving the collective action problems these norms represent, may be resolved if the rewards and punishments concerned require unanimous or near-unanimous agreement and cooperation in order to be produced. Norms thus serve to reduce sets of collective action problems, which are unlikely to be resolved, to a single collective action problem, norm-enforcement, which is more likely to be resolved. The more nearly unanimous the agreement required to enact the rewards and punishments involved, the more effective this solution.

THE NORM OF HONESTY

If everyone in a particular group adhered to a norm of honesty, then they might well be able to cooperate over the production of other, more tangible, collective consumption goods, as each would be confident that others would keep their side of any bargains made. Adherence to this norm would be encouraged by a system of social rewards and punishments, similar to the one described above. Three criteria would have to be fulfilled.

Firstly, the group would need an unambiguous definition of 'dishonesty', agreed by all. This, in turn, places certain constraints upon the form of agreement to which the norm of honesty can be applied. It creates a need either for disinterested witnesses to verbal agreements, or for more tangible evidence, such as written statements. It would be almost impossible for a particular verbal, unwitnessed, agreement between two interested parties to be the object of a collective judgement by the group, since there would be no objective record of the agreement which could be used as a yardstick against which the subsequent behaviour of the interested parties could be judged. Indeed, even the witnessing of a verbal agreement by a 'disinterested' party might present problems, since it would always be possible for the motives of the witness to be impugned. While written statements may also, of course, be falsified, it would probably be more straightforward to devise some system which rendered this possibility less likely. (The signature of both parties on a piece of 'safety' paper, which would clearly indicate attempts to tamper with it, might suffice.)

The second necessary criterion for group adherence to a norm of honesty is that defectors can be identified. This poses further constraints upon the nature of the agreement which such a norm might encompass. For example, it would tend to restrict such agreements to the realm of *observable behaviour*, as opposed to *intent*, since it would be almost impossible to demonstrate deviation from even an unambiguous declaration of intent.

Finally, the group would need to have at its disposal a sanction which would both be sufficient to encourage potential defectors to cooperate, and be such that the enactment of the sanction would not present the group with an insoluble second-order collective action problem. We have already seen, for example, that the exclusion of recalcitrants from the group might fulfil this function, since this sanction involves almost total jointness of production.

The full exploration of the social dynamics of a norm of honesty would go far beyond the scope of this book. (Indeed it would fill another book.) We can see, however, that, in certain circumstances, a group of rational individuals might 'anarchistically' adhere to such a norm, and thus facilitate the provision of other collective consumption goods. Anarchistic honesty may not look very honest, but it may nevertheless be adhered to with respect to written or witnessed agreements concerning observable behaviour, and be backed up by a collective sanction, such as exclusion from the group.

IN CONCLUSION

We have seen that, while rational men may well desire public goods, they will have some trouble providing these if they always behave according to the dictates of selfish utility-maximization. This creates a problem of market failure in these goods, to which there are a number of potential solutions. In the first place, the problem may solve itself, if the goods in question are such that they require the unanimous cooperation of consumers in order to be produced at all. In the second place, some goods may be easily 'privatized' by the adoption of cheap and simple exclusion mechanisms. In the third place, public goods may be produced anyway, as externalities to private transactions. In none of these cases do we really have a problem, and we may wish to think of the 'real' collective action problem as applying to those public goods to which these potential solutions do not apply. These would be goods requiring some, but not total, jointness of production; goods which it is difficult or expensive to exclude people from consuming; and goods which are not produced as a spin-off from other activity.

The provision of these goods may be facilitated by a strong ruler who forced people to keep their promises. But we must assume that such an individual is disinterested in the goals being realized by his 'clientele'; otherwise he will become a dictator. Failing a saint, or a god whose function was the disinterested punishment of man-made rules, there are some goods which may be provided by groups of individuals on a 'self-policing', or anarchistic, basis. We have seen that these tend to be goods involving the modification of behaviour, and might well include norms, such as honesty, which would greatly facilitate the provision of other collective goods.

Notwithstanding all of this, there are still many categories of public good, particularly those involving large-scale social investment, which we have yet to account for. The next chapter considers these, and the role of political entrepreneurs in their provision.

POLITICAL ENTREPRENEURS

The production of public goods can also be achieved by an entrepreneur who sets up in the business of supplying them at a profit. If the total value attached to a good by members of a group is greater than the cost of providing it, then a potential surplus exists for anyone who can produce the good in exchange for contributions from consumers. Each individual will be prepared to contribute an amount equal to or less than the utility derived from the good in question. This surplus is available to an entrepreneur, whether or not the entrepreneur derives any utility from the good produced. While the incentives to entrepreneurs to move into this market are clear, the contributions of consumers need to be explained. Whether or not members of the group make these payments, they can consume the public goods produced. Four possible explanations have been suggested, which can be taken as a starting-point for this argument.[1]

Firstly, an entrepreneur can try to convince consumers that a particular collective consumption good is more likely to be produced as a direct consequence of his or her activities.[2] If nobody organizes the production of the good, we have seen that some consumers may be prepared to make some small contribution towards production costs. These people value the good sufficiently highly that they are prepared to unilaterally underwrite at least a modest level of production. Even if nobody else contributes, their high valuation of the good makes it worth while for them to provide a small amount of it, regardless of the fact that it is then enjoyed free of charge by others. The entrepreneur has nothing to offer these voluntary contributors, however, and is still vulnerable to free riders. Rational individuals will not make or increase voluntary contributions towards the costs of providing public goods, just because the goods are now provided by an entrepreneur. The entrepreneur does not increase the *specific probability* that the contribution made by an individual will produce a *directly consequential increase* in utility income.

This probability is the crux of the collective action problem. It is only by increasing the chance that a *specific* donation will *directly* produce a private benefit to the donor that the probability of such donations can be increased. The entrepreneur does not achieve this by setting up a collection organization, and does not therefore increase the probability that donations will be made. Entrepreneurs will be ignored by the few who value the good highly enough to make donations anyway, since they will be consuming resources without providing anything in return. As they do not increase the chance that the public good will be produced, there is no reason why consumers need have anything to do with them. Entrepreneurs may, of course, agree to supply the public good in exchange for funds from those who would contribute unconditionally. In this case, they are acting quite simply as private contractors engaged in private transactions with those who wish the good supplied. These consumers treat the good as if it were a private good. Indeed, such arrangements will only be effective when jointness of production is low. The only difference between this and a wholly private transaction is that production of the good has externalities which are regarded as a public good by non-contributors. The good is collectively consumed as a public good, but produced as a private good. In any case, the whole point of the collective action problem is that, except in the very smallest groups, only a very limited production of public goods will take place. If the whole cost of the good has to be underwritten by one particularly keen individual, the level of resources forthcoming will be so small that the good in question will be greatly underprovided. An entrepreneur does not alter this situation, and therefore provides no solution to the collective action problem, by offering to organize the production of collective consumption goods on the basis of voluntary contributions.

A second possible source of income for an entrepreneur is the group of potential suppliers of factors of production for the collective goods in question.[3] Most public goods will consist of several factors of production, and many of these will themselves be private goods. The private factors of production of public goods will obviously have to be supplied from somewhere. Some suppliers may well come from within the group of consumers of the public good. These suppliers may make contributions in the hope of increasing their chances of making profitable private supply contracts with the entrepreneur. However, the fact that some members of the group will derive additional private benefits in the form of supply contracts if the public good is produced does not overcome the collective action problem. The entrepreneur will wish to purchase factors of production as cheaply as possible, regardless of whether or not the supplier is also a contributor. Restricting supply contracts to contributors cannot possibly finance a public good, since the profits to be made from supplying the factors of production must obviously be less than the total cost of producing the good. The total cannot therefore be met by contributions from rational suppliers.

The only possible exception to this is if entrepreneurs start playing games with their potential suppliers. They might declare that, regardless of cost, they will only purchase the goods from contributors. This amounts to a bluff, which can be called by potential suppliers. They can refuse to contribute, and force public entrepreneurs to purchase factors of production, at high prices, from contributors (who may well jack up these prices to cover the cost of contributions). Entrepreneurs would win this game by holding out the carrot of probable contracts to potential suppliers, and encouraging more of them to contribute than can be rewarded with contracts. They would then make a profit out of the surplus contributions of unlucky potential suppliers. Some contributors would receive profitable supply contracts, but others would not. The entrepreneur's profit in this instance is made entirely as a result of outsmarting potential suppliers.

A third method of raising revenue for collective consumption goods is taxation.[4] Entrepreneurs can set up a system of sanctions to enforce an agreed 'contribution' from all consumers. They can punish recalcitrants by enforcing a penalty which exceeds the cost of the contribution required. This dramatically alters the cost-benefit calculations of potential free-riders. It becomes more costly to withhold contributions than to make them. Even if the *enactment* of any particular sanction costs more than the contribution which it was designed to elicit, the *threat* of sanctions may well encourage the others to contribute. Actually carrying out costly sanctions from time to time will therefore be worthwhile. This method of raising revenue can be used to finance any type of collective consumption good, since it does not depend at all upon excluding anyone. The sanctions can be completely separated from the good itself. In nother words, the entrepreneurs offer members of the group a contract, providing public goods in exchange for contributions which yield them a private surplus. They collect revenue on the basis of a coercive power of taxation, which is granted by the group *conditionally* upon satisfactory provision of the goods in question. In order to avoid the problem that an unscrupulous entrepreneur with the power to coerce the whole group would presumably collect the money and refuse to provide any collective goods, it should be clear that the powers of taxation granted by the group must only give an entrepreneur the ability to coerce *individual* recalcitrants. Power to coerce the group *en masse* would make the entrepreneur a potential dictator.

A final possibility is 'extortion'.[5] This involves the entrepreneur threatening to impose sanctions on the group *as a whole* rather than on individuals, if an agreed level of contributions is not forthcoming. This makes a group's failure to provide resources for the collective good into an explicit public bad. The threat of general punishment will be effective only in certain circumstances, however. Both the minimum level of contributions which triggers reprisals, and the actual current level of contributions being made by the group, must be known to every member. If this is not the case, then free-riders will defect anyway. If these parameters are known, then free-riders will defect until the minimum level is reached. At that point, any further failure to contribute triggers group punishment. This makes further contributions quite rational. The minimum level of contributions which triggers sanctions is, of course, entirely arbitrary. It will thus, presumably, be set as high as possible by the entrepreneur. The higher the level is set, the greater the proportion of the group that is forced to contribute, and thus the greater the jointness of production of the public good 'avoiding punishment'. Entrepreneurs thus 'help' the group to produce the collective consumption goods it desires by tying together two collective goods, one of which (punishment) is within their control and exhibits high jointness of production, and is thus less susceptible to free-riding.

Extortion may or may not be preferred by the entrepreneur to taxation. The former may be cheaper, if identifying individual defectors is costly but sanctions are cheap. In this case, many of the costs of coercion are hived off onto the group itself. The group can police itself in order to avoid collective sanctions, either by additional collective action (of an anarchistic nature), or on the basis of individual freelance 'vigilante' action. In these circumstances, a rather sophisticated form of free-rider problem is likely to appear. Since each member of the group pays the price if a missing contribution is neither enforced nor made up by the others, potential free-riders who deem the chance of being identified to be small can defect, in the confident expectation that any shortfall will be made up by their colleagues.

One point, however, is quite clear. A group of rational individuals will never give another rational individual the power to coerce the whole group, which is necessary for extortion. There is no reason for them to suppose that this power will not be used to exploit them mercilessly. The group will have no recourse against an entrepreneur to whom they have given the power to coerce them all. Such entrepreneurs would have no need to produce any public goods, since they could raise revenue by coercion whether they produced them or not. An entrepreneur who had the power to coerce the group *en masse* would be a dictator, and we have already seen that it can never be rational for a group to submit itself to a dictator. Thus, the only arrangement which is attractive both to entrepreneurs and to 'clients' is one which provides the entrepreneur with sanctions to enforce *individual* contributions, and hence counteract rational tendencies to take free rides. It would not be rational for entrepreneurs to go into business expecting to raise revenue from voluntary conditional contributions. Of the alternatives discussed, taxation is the only basic source of revenue acceptable to all parties. Although contributions from hopeful subcontractors may provide a welcome bonus for entrepreneurs, they could never provide collective goods on the basis of these alone.

The grant of coercive power to the entrepreneur is, of course, conditional upon satisfactory provision of agreed levels of public goods. The relationship between political entrepreneur and client thus takes the form of a 'contract'. The contract will specify the powers granted to the entrepreneur, the levels of taxation to be enforced and the desired level of production of public goods. The contract ceases to be binding upon failure to deliver by either side. Since members of the group will never rationally grant an entrepreneur the power to coerce them all, both sides are in a position to repudiate the contract whenever they so desire. In deciding whether or not to repudiate this contract, both sides, but particularly the consumers, will have to face some complex strategic decisions. Entrepreneurs, concerned to maximize their profits, are likely to under-perform, producing smaller quantities of public goods than those agreed in their contract with the public. They can do this in the knowledge that, as long as they are producing a sufficiently high level of public goods for most people to be realizing a surplus on their tax payments, then the population is unlikely to repudiate the contract. However, even a monopolistic political entrepreneur can be forced to produce public goods, if the marginal cost of coercing recalcitrant individuals exceeds the marginal benefits. If producing below an agreed level yields a net loss (because of high coercion costs), the possibility of consumer resistance will lead a monopolistic entrepreneur to produce public goods at close to agreed levels. Thus, rational entrepreneurs may honour their public goods contracts with consumers in those circumstances where dishonouring them provokes consumer resistance and potentially heavy losses.

Albert Hirschman extensively explores a related problem in *Exit, Voice and Loyalty*.[6] While he does not consider entrepreneurs' *coercion costs*, Hirschman does argue that market mechanisms may be partially replaced, for public goods, by the consequences of consumer resistance. When consumers who desire public goods are 'locked' into the system – in our terms, when revenue is raised on a coercive basis – then their only response to a decline in output is to complain, to use their Voice. A rational entrepreneur responds to Voice, not because he or she wants to, but because it is costly to ignore it. This is mainly because continuing noisy complaints from some dissatisfied consumers are likely to alert other – less sensitive or more apathetic – consumers to what is going on.[7] Our argument demonstrates why Hirschman's entrepreneurs would be concerned about this. If the level of consumer dissatisfaction influences entrepreneurs' coercion costs, and if a certain level of coercion costs renders continued entrepreneurial activities unprofitable, then the Voice of a sensitive consumer may be quite effective. Although it might be perfectly possible for entrepreneurs to coerce sensitive consumers into paying their taxes, their noisy complaints about the declining quality of public goods provision threaten even higher coercion costs in the future, as others become dissatisfied. If these complaints are likely to alert sufficient consumers for the entrepreneur to be faced with an unprofitable level of coercion, then there will be an incentive to find an alternative response to the original complaint. Thus, Voice may elicit a response from entrepreneurs. It should be clear, however, that actually fulfilling contractual obligations is only one of several possible responses. Entrepreneurs could pay off complainants privately, or find a more sinister means of silencing them.

A more significant constraint upon the entrepreneur is the threat posed by rivals and opponents. The contract to supply public goods to the group will be profitable, and will thus be coveted by others, who will offer competing packages to members of the group in the hope of attracting their patronage. Some writers have argued that, since opposition of this sort is a public good for the group as a whole, opposition can itself become a career. Rival entrepreneurs realize a surplus simply by supplying the good of opposition.[8] This is incoherent for two reasons. Firstly, rivals and opponents will hardly be in a position to use taxation as a method of raising revenue; yet no member of the group will *voluntarily* contribute towards the costs of a rival entrepreneur, simply in order to increase the public good of 'competition'. (Since competition is a public good, it will be subject to free-riding, like all public goods.) The second problem is that, although a rival entrepreneur produces the collective good of competition, it is also clear that any attempt to make a living solely on the basis of supplying this good falls prey to the most peculiar paradoxes. The value of the collective good produced by the competitor is almost equal to that produced by the incumbent. This is because the incumbent would hardly produce public goods at all if there was no threat of competition, but is forced by this threat to honour agreements made. Despite producing this valuable public good, the costs of the rival entrepreneur would be much lower than those of the incumbent, since no tangible good would have to be produced. The only real costs of the rival entrepreneur would be those necessary to stay alive and maintain a challenge. Thus, the surplus which would be realized by a rival who had some way of collecting resources on the basis of providing the good of opposition would be much larger than the surplus which could be realized by the incumbent. The two would be competing *not* to be the incumbent. The threat of competition would therefore act as no constraint upon the incumbent.

These problems disappear once we reject all methods of raising the revenue to finance a challenge to the incumbent on the basis of producing the collective good of opposition. Instead, the rival entrepreneur must be regarded as someone who makes a private investment in the potential benefits to be received from contracting with the group to supply public goods. No pay-off accrues to a rival from being in opposition, just as competitors in private goods markets receive no pay-off simply for providing (the public good of) competition. However, if the rival entrepreneur has a real chance of making contracts to supply the group with public goods, another source of finance is available. Aspiring suppliers of factors of production may contribute on the basis of promises to reward them with profitable contracts once the rival becomes the incumbent. While potential suppliers, for obvious reasons, can never fully finance the incumbent, aspiring suppliers can fully finance a *challenger*, since the costs of opposition will be much less. Suppliers will only do this, of course, if they expect the rival entrepreneur to prevail and eventually secure the public goods contract. Aspiring suppliers will obviously not fund someone who makes a *career* of opposition. Thus, if a rival entrepreneur is making a serious attempt to take over the incumbency, the challenge can be financed on the basis of contributions from aspirant suppliers. It will clearly also act as a constraint upon the incumbent. This is the only form of opposition which receives any financial support. Support is forthcoming, not because rival entrepreneurs provide the public good of opposition, but because they are potential dispensers of patronage.

The threat posed by rivals is clearly going to involve the incumbent in competition costs. Responses must be produced to the package offered by opponents, and constructing and publicizing these responses will cost resources. The incumbent may deploy resources from the surplus generated by public goods contracts, of course, but will additionally be able to ask for contributions from the current suppliers of factors of production. These will have an interest in keeping the incumbent in office, since they will not want to lose their profitable supply contracts. The incumbent may be able to match the opposition in terms of competition costs, since both the incumbent and the suppliers can finance these from cash flow, and do not have to make the risky investment required of challengers and their supporters. However, rival entrepreneurs may well attempt to seduce some of the backers of the incumbent by offering them a better deal once the incumbent is ousted. Since the incumbent is forced to deal in reality, support comes only from those who are actually paid off. Rivals can deal in promises, and may be able to recruit a larger number of backers than they will actually be able to satisfy when the time comes to issue contracts. This makes the mounting of viable opposition relatively easy, since the costs involved will be rather small when compared with the potential benefits to hopeful suppliers of factors of production.

THE NATURE OF COMPETITION FOR
PUBLIC GOODS CONTRACTS

We have just seen that, although monopolistic entrepreneurs may produce some public goods in order to avert the damaging consequences of consumer resistance, it is the threat of competition from rival entrepreneurs which greatly increases incentives to honour public goods contracts. The precise nature of this competition may well be different, however, from that of competition over private goods contracts, because of the very nature of public goods. With private goods, competition can take the form of 'simultaneous provision' of similar or identical goods by a number of competing entrepreneurs. Because, by definition, it is possible to exclude people from the consumption of private goods, simultaneous provision presents no problems. Each entrepreneur has a group of clients with whom private goods contracts are made. If any clients refuse to meet the obligations of this contract, they can be prevented from consuming the good. The sanctions operated by private entrepreneurs are passive, and two or more entrepreneurs can therefore operate these sanctions simultaneously without necessarily coming into conflict with each other.

We have also seen that goods may exhibit a fair degree of 'publicness', yet still be such that it is possible to exclude people from consuming them. An example of this type of good is a public park, which is jointly supplied to a group of consumers, despite the fact that it is possible to exercise control over the membership of that group. Entrepreneurs may produce such goods and realize a surplus, on the basis of their ability to exclude recalcitrants from consumption of benefits towards which they have not contributed. In these cases, therefore, simultaneous provision of similar public goods by rival entrepreneurs is perfectly possible, since the passive sanctions involved imply no necessary conflict between them. Two or more entrepreneurs could thus set up rival public parks, police forces or fire brigades simultaneously, and compete with each other on the basis of providing the good to those who were prepared to contribute to production costs, while excluding those who were not.

Many public goods are such, however, that it is not economically feasible to exclude specified individuals from their consumption. We saw in the previous section that a public entrepreneur may realize a surplus from the production of 'non-excludable' goods only on the basis of some form of coercion. In these cases, simultaneous provision of similar goods by rival entrepreneurs presents severe problems. These arise because, while it is easy to envisage sanctions which may be directed against *any* particular individual, it is much harder to imagine sanctions which may be directed *only* against members of a predetermined group of individuals. Such sanctions may, of course, exist in certain special cases. Members of a group of drug addicts may each be totally dependent on the supply of a particular substance which is controlled by an entrepreneur. The Man may make a contract with them to supply a particular public good in exchange for contributions from them. If any withholds the contribution, then the Man can withhold the drug. Yet this sanction would only apply to the group of addicts; it would be totally irrelevant to anyone who was not an addict. Examples of this type of person-specific sanction will, however, be the exception rather than the rule. In any case, there is absolutely no guarantee that the group of consumers to which the sanction applies will correspond to the group of people wanting to make a public goods contract with the entrepreneur.

When the sanctions at the disposal of rival entrepreneurs cannot be applied only to predetermined individuals, and when these entrepreneurs are simultaneously providing similar or identical public goods, there is almost bound to be serious conflict. There is no reason to suppose that each entrepreneur will not attempt to impose sanctions upon the clients of rivals, as well as upon his or her own clients, in an attempt to force contributions from them. Indeed, it may also be in the interest of an entrepreneur's existing clients for the clients of rival entrepreneurs to be subjected to these sanctions; any who are thus encouraged to join the fold may reduce the costs borne by those already there. Competition between entrepreneurs will thus be just as likely to involve punishing rivals' clients as improving their own performance. The incentives to improve performance will furthermore be reduced by the knowledge

that those consumers who take their custom elsewhere can be co-
erced anyway. Competition between entrepreneurs simultaneously
providing non-excludable public goods on the basis of contributions backed up by sanctions will thus place a heavy burden
on members of the group. They may be punished, whether or not
they are recalcitrant, by someone with whom they have no contract. Also, this competition, unlike competition over the production of excludable goods, provides no mechanism for improving the
performance of the competitors, since each need not automatically
lose resources to rivals when their own performance declines. In
short, the market failure represented by the collective action problem works both ways. Not only do producers need to find some
alternative method of raising revenue to meet their costs, but consumers need some way of ensuring that producers maintain maximum efficiency. Competition on the basis of simultaneous
provision is likely not to involve the continuing attempt to offer
consumers the best deal.

An alternative mode of competition is 'sequential monopoly'.
Under this arrangement, a fixed-term public goods contract is put
out for tender to rival entrepreneurs and awarded, exclusively, to
the entrepreneur submitting the best tender. When the fixed term
expires, the contract is put out for tender once more, and the
process is repeated. This arrangement forces the entrepreneur to
honour contractual obligations, for fear of losing the public goods
contract when it is resubmitted for tender. Furthermore, it does not
involve the costs to each group member of competitive simultaneous provision. Each member will be subject to a contract with a
single entrepreneur and, at worst, can expect to be on the receiving
end of a single set of sanctions if he or she is recalcitrant. Each
group member will furthermore have a good idea of what is likely
to be interpreted as recalcitrant behaviour. (When rival entrepreneurs are simultaneously in the field, one of them will always
be thinking that the other's clients are recalcitrant, and punishing
them.) Either way, the costs of simultaneous competition are
greater than those of sequential monopoly.

This argument will apply not only to the provision of similar or
identical public goods, but also to all public goods not susceptible to

the exclusion of recalcitrants, unless the sanctions at the disposal of the entrepreneurs concerned can be so restricted as to apply *only* to the good in question. A collection of monopolistic entrepreneurs producing different non-excludable public goods will be just as much in competition with each other as rival entrepreneurs simultaneously producing the same good. They will each be looking for ways to increase their surplus, however this is generated, and will therefore covet other profitable exclusive public goods contracts. Such competition between rival monopolists producing different public goods will impose costs on all concerned, including consumers, unless some way can be found of limiting the scope of sanctions to apply only in the case of those who are recalcitrant with respect to *specific* public goods contracts. These costs can be avoided by awarding fixed-term monopolistic contracts for the provision of *all* desired non-excludable public goods to a single entrepreneur. This would limit the competitive use of sanctions by rival entrepreneurs, while at the same time ensuring some form of competition necessary to control the performance of the incumbent. At any one time, therefore, there would be a single incumbent, producing all desired non-excludable goods, who would have a fixed-term contract with his clientele.

AWARDING PUBLIC GOODS CONTRACTS

The use of the word 'contract' in this context is possibly a little misleading, since a contract is usually an agreement which carries the force of law. However, a legal system will be one of the non-excludable public goods up for tender. With respect to this contract at least, there can be no independent legal enforcement, since the enforcer will be one of the parties to the agreement. The contract which includes an obligation to maintain a legal system cannot carry the force of law to any meaningful extent. In this particular context, therefore, the methods of ensuring that contracts are fulfilled are rather more down-to-earth, resting on good old-fashioned force. Contracts will be observed to the extent that they are backed up by a credible threat, available to all parties, of sanctions. The entrepreneurs concerned possess the ability, as well as the consent of their clientele, to enforce sanctions against individual recalcitrants. This is part of the essence of the public goods contract. Entrepreneurs do not, however, possess the ability to coerce the group *en masse*. Collectively, therefore, the group will be able to impose its will on an entrepreneur. This imposition of will itself involves collective action, however; we must therefore be sure that it will be possible for such corporate enforcement to take place.

There are two possible methods for producing the collective enforcement of contracts. The first arises from competition between entrepreneurs. A rival, using personal resources, or backed by aspirant suppliers of factors of production, may underwrite collective enforcement costs in exchange for subsequent public goods contracts. Secondly, collective action against recalcitrant entrepreneurs may be organized anarchistically, along the lines discussed earlier. This may well be feasible, since the removal of a particular recalcitrant incumbent will be an 'all-or-nothing' good for the group. The minimum level of provision of this goal which can be secured by the group, if the conditions for arriving at anarchistic agreement obtain, will be sufficient for the purpose at hand.

In each of these cases, contracts with public entrepreneurs are enforced by coercion or the threat of coercion. If the members of the group wish to retain their credibility to threaten future recalcitrants with force if agreements are not honoured, then they may accept the use of force in a particular circumstance, even when the costs involved exceed the benefits. This will be for precisely the same reasons that anarchistic groups will wind up profitable agreements in the face of recalcitrance. Each group must include the increased probability that other profitable contracts will be honoured in any evaluation of the benefits of coercing a specific recalcitrant. If members of the group let one particular entrepreneur get away with double-crossing them, everyone else will try and do the same thing. Since they have to make a stand somewhere, they might as well make it as soon as they are double-crossed. Thus, disposing of an unsatisfactory entrepreneur will involve costs. These costs will be either financed by a rival, or raised anarchistically.

From this it follows that members of a sub-group which controls a majority of the coercive capacity in the group in question will find it rational to enter into contracts with public entrepreneurs for the production of valued, non-excludable goods. They will do this in the confident expectation that these contracts will be honoured, since, if they are not honoured, any group which controls a majority of the coercive resources can *enforce* them.

Members of sub-groups which do not control a majority of the coercive resources may find themselves in this position, in certain special circumstances, if they control more coercive resources than any other sub-group which shares common goals. If the remaining members of the population are sufficiently diverse in their aspirations as to be unlikely to unite in opposition to the sub-group in question, then members of the strongest sub-group in the system may be able to impose their will, whether or not they control a majority of the coercive resources. Diversity of aspirations has two aspects. First, with respect to particular goals, the remaining members of the population may have preferences such that there is no sub-group which could possibly form which both controls more resources than the original sub-group, and also prefers a *particular* alternative outcome. Thus, a group which controls, say, 40 per cent of the coercive resources will be able to enforce a contract to produce a medium-sized public park if, of the remaining 60 per cent, half would prefer a small park and half a large one.

Secondly, since the increased credibility to make future agreements is one of the benefits of enforcing a particular agreement, members of sub-groups who share more goals in common will be more inclined to enforce agreements than members of sub-groups who share fewer goals in common. Members of the latter sub-groups will perceive fewer benefits arising from imposing a particular outcome, even at a loss, and they would therefore be less likely to do so. Thus, the members of one group, simply drawn together by their common desire for clean air, might control more coercive resources than, but still be no match for, a group whose members shared a vast range of common interests. The latter group might oppose the spending of resources on clean air; but it would not be worth the stronger group imposing a particular contract at a loss, once coercion costs were considered. There would be nothing against which a group without other shared interests could offset this loss. The group with many fish to fry might decide that this particular loss was worth bearing, in order to make it clear that they mean business. The air would stay dirty, despite the fact that the more powerful group wanted it clean. It would stay dirty because the group which prefers dirty air has more at stake in getting its own way. Other things being equal, the more shared goals a particular sub-group has, the more formidable an opponent it will prove to be.

Whatever happens, the sub-group which has the effective power to impose its own will finds it rational to make public goods contracts with a political entrepreneur. If we make no specific assumptions about the distribution of goals between groups, this will tend to be the group controlling a majority of the coercive resources. Particular distributions of goals may modify this conclusion. The more equal the distribution of coercive resources in the whole group, the more any sub-group with a majority of coercive resources will approximate in size to a majority of the total population. The less information that exists about the distribution of coercive resources, the more realistic it is for a group with a majority of the population to assume that it controls a majority of the coercive resources. (This information may well become less clear-cut as group size increases.) Finally, the more diverse the interests of the population, the less likely it is that any group which is not a majority of the population will have the effective power to impose its own will. This is because it is community, rather than diversity, of interest which enables a less powerful group to impose its will on a more powerful one.

These conclusions are subject to a very important exception, however, which arises as a result of the structure of preferences which certain goods and issues will produce in the group. It is possible that certain issues which have three or more independent resolutions will be such that there is no sub-group in the population which both controls a majority of the coercive resources and clearly prefers one resolution to all others. For example, if there are three basic sub-groups, defined by their preferences on a particular issue, none of which controls a majority, but any two of which

control a majority between them, it is a simple matter to construct
a set of preference orderings with respect to the resolutions of the
issue which has the property that, for *any* resolution, there is
always an alternative which is preferred by a more powerful coalition of groups. Let the three groups prefer policies which devote
the majority of tax revenue to defence, to the environment, and to
public health respectively. Let the first group rank these alternatives in the order: defence, environment and health; let the second
group rank them: environment, health and defence; and let the
third group rank them: health, defence and environment. (This set
of preference orderings is referred to as 'cyclical'.) If two rival entrepreneurs support the defence and environment packages respectively, then the defence package will prevail, since two sub-groups
prefer defence to environment. However, the entrepreneur offering
the environment package could switch to the health package, and
secure the allegiance of the two groups who prefer health to defence. The entrepreneur offering defence could now switch to
offering the environment package, and secure the support of the
two groups who prefer environment to health. The cycle would be
completed when the entrepreneur offering the health package
switched to the defence package, and attracted the support of the
two groups preferring defence to the environment. The choice
would once more be between defence and the environment,
and the whole process could start all over again. There is no single
package which always commands the support of a coalition controlling a majority of the power in the group. Any given majority
coalition can be destroyed by selecting a particular alternative
package. This problem has been of considerable recent concern to
rational choice theorists, and is usually referred to as the paradox
of voting, or the problem of cyclical majorities.[9] 'If nothing was
done about it', this structure of preferences in the group would
result in entrepreneurs continuously changing their policies, with
the particular contract which emerged being determined by the
chance pair of packages which happened to be on offer when the
time for a final decision arrived. This problem is of limited concern
to us here, since we are not concerned with the 'efficiency' or 'social
rationality' of decisions which are taken by the group. We should

note, however, that a cyclical structure of preferences in the group, of the type described, will mean that contracts will be less likely to be enforced anarchistically by the group. Such a structure of preferences will always give rise to a situation where there will be a group in the population which has both the desire and the ability to destroy any particular contract which is agreed. Cyclical preferences will, in short, make for much greater instability.

Considerable energy has been devoted to exploring those circumstances in which this instability is avoided. Most conclusions on this matter depend upon some sort of assumption of limited coherence in the preferences of the group. Such assumptions are usually designed to reduce the potency of the effect of cyclical sets of preferences. Obviously, if there is a group with a majority of the coercive resources which prefers a single resolution of the issue concerned, then the paradox does not arise, and that resolution will prevail. A particular resolution will be dominant in other circumstances, however. If the previous example is modified so that the three groups prefer the alternatives in the respective orders (defence, environment, health), (health, defence, environment) and (environment, defence, health), then any entrepreneur offering the defence package will be able to make a stable contract with a coalition of groups which does control a majority of the coercive resources. This is because there is no alternative package which is preferred to defence by a majority coalition, and is despite the fact that defence is not ranked first by a majority coalition. The only strategy open to a rival in these circumstances would be to offer a very similar package, and to look for details which made the rival package marginally more attractive than the one offered by the incumbent. We can see, however, that the modified structure of preference orderings reflects rather more consensus in the group than was previously the case, since defence is ranked last by no one in the group. Many attempts have been made to determine minimum conditions for this stability of social choice. Nearly all rely on the assumption of some limited form of consensus or, in Sen's terms, they rely on 'value-restrictedness'.[10] We will return to a fuller justification of the plausibility of such an assumption in Chapter 5.

In the most general terms, therefore, we can say no more than that stable, fixed-term, exclusive contracts to produce public goods will be awarded by a sub-group, or coalition of sub-groups, which controls a majority of coercive resources. We have seen that the stability of these contracts may be undermined when members of the group have very divergent preferences. We have also seen that there will be an increasing tendency for the group which controls a majority of the coercive resources to approximate to a majority of the population as the distribution of coercive resources becomes more even, as information about this distribution decreases, and as diversity of interest increases. Majority decisions on the award of contracts will thus tend to be more stable in large groups when coercive resources are distributed more evenly – or less predictably – and when preferences are relatively diverse, while retaining some underlying coherence. They will be less stable in small groups with skewed distributions of resources which have either highly polarized preferences or the fundamental lack of consensus represented by cyclical sets of preference orderings.

COLLUSION AND COMPETITION

While competition between rival entrepreneurs will provide some control over their output, public entrepreneurs will have the same incentives to collude as the suppliers of private goods. If competition can be restricted, and the range of alternative options available to consumers limited, the entrepreneurs' surplus can be increased. Both the potential for, and the profits from, collusion will increase as the number of competing entrepreneurs decreases. The incumbent will still have to offer a public goods contract which yields a surplus for some sub-group of consumers controlling a majority of the coercive resources. However, as long as such a surplus is provided, no more than this will need to be offered if the incumbent faces no competition. Competition presents the incumbent with the prospect of producing much higher levels of public goods than this bare minimum. The potential therefore exists for the making of side-payments to potential competitors which are conditional upon their quiescence. It will be rational to accept a side-payment as long as its value exceeds the potential surplus available to the challenger on becoming the incumbent. In a competitive environment, the surplus available to the incumbent will be much smaller than that available in the absence of competition. It is therefore quite possible that the *additional* surplus available to the incumbent in the absence of competition will exceed the *total* surplus available with full competition. If this condition is satisfied, then the incumbent will have both the incentive and the resources to buy off a competitor, and the competitor would be quite rational to accept the payment.

The number of potential competitors will influence the potential for collusion, since each potential competitor will require the same payment. For a given increase in profit arising from restricting competition, there will be a greater number of rivals who need to be bought off and a lower probability that such pay-offs will be rational for the incumbent. This is because the increase in profit is completely independent of the number of rivals. We have already seen that two factors affect the rationality of financing a challenger, and hence affect the number of potential challengers. Challengers either finance themselves, regarding their costs as an investment in the potential rewards of incumbency, or they are financed by aspiring suppliers of factors of production. The more group members there are with the resources to challenge the incumbent, and the more aspiring suppliers of factors of production there are, the more challengers there are likely to be. The more challengers, the less likely is collusion between 'rival' entrepreneurs.

Just as the size of the barriers to entry is one of the most important factors affecting collusion in private goods markets, so the level of costs involved in challenging an incumbent will affect the potential for collusion in the public goods market. The higher these costs, the more likely is collusion. Furthermore, to the extent that the factors of production of public goods are in themselves private goods, the number of potential financiers of competition in the public goods market (and hence the number of potential competitors) will depend on the number of competitors in the private goods market. The more oligopolistic the private goods market, the fewer the potential patrons of rival entrepreneurs, and hence the greater the possibility of collusion.

The second factor which affects the potential for collusion is the level of additional surplus which can be realized. This will depend upon the relationships between the total cost of producing the goods in question, and the maximum aggregate benefit derived from those goods by any subset of the group controlling a majority of the coercive resources. The more intense the competition, the more the income from a given level of production will approach total costs, as competitors vie with each other to submit the most attractive tender. A single entrepreneur with no competition, however, can extract contributions approaching the maximum aggregate value of the good. The greater the gap between production costs and evaluation of the goods in question, the greater the scope for collusion. The size of this gap will depend on the specific goods produced, and their evaluation by a particular group. For a given set of goods, however, the cost *per consumer* of providing the good may well decrease with the increasing size of the group. Some 'all-or-nothing' goods will have to be provided, and provided in a fixed quantity, whatever the size of the group, while many other goods will exhibit economies of scale. In these cases, the gap between production costs and consumer evaluation will grow as the size of the group grows. For sets of public goods with this property, the potential for collusion will therefore increase as the group gets larger (although other factors, such as the number of potential competitors, will tend to counteract this).

Collusion has, in this discussion, been considered solely in the form of side-payments. Side-payments, however, need merely to be viewed as a measure of the *potential* for all types of collusion. Of course, such payments are likely to be disapproved of by nearly every member of the group, since they always reflect a reduction in the surplus available to consumers. However, the *potential* for collusion, reflected in the potential for side-payments, need not be consummated by the vulgar and public exchange of hard cash. Side-payments may, of course, be secret. More importantly however, surplus may be transferred from donor to recipient by a multitude of other means. The donor may offer a 'knock-for-knock' agreement, ceding certain profitable sections of the market to the recipient. Alternatively, the donor may produce a public goods package which is more favourable to the recipient than would otherwise have been the case, award private supply contracts for factors of production, or indulge in any one of the galaxy of other methods for effectively transferring resources from one party to another.

To sum up, the potential for collusion in the public goods market will depend on the number of potential competitors in that market. This will in turn depend on the costs of mounting a credible challenge, the distribution of resources in the group, the degree of competition in the private goods market and the nature of the goods involved. The higher the cost of challenging the incumbent, the more unequal the distribution of resources, the lower the level of competition in the private goods market and the more highly the goods in question are valued relative to production costs, then the greater the potential for collusion between supposedly rival public entrepreneurs.

THE CONSUMPTION SURPLUS OF ENTREPRENEURS

Most discussions by rational choice theorists of the role of political entrepreneurs quite explicitly rule out consideration of the influence of the intrinsic private preferences of politicians.[11] Public entrepreneurs are viewed as being entirely instrumental, producing packages of public goods with no concern for their own preferences. They are in business to make a profit, and do not care where that profit comes from. This rules out the possibility that entrepreneurs are in business in order to promote *particular* packages of public goods for reasons of their own. Their rewards are assumed to arise from producing, rather than consuming, public goods.

Consider the consumption surplus of entrepreneurs, however. They will derive consumption benefits to the extent that they produce public goods packages which are closer to the ones they would privately prefer than those which would otherwise emerge. Of course, increasing profits from production may well decrease entrepreneurs' private consumption, as there is no guarantee that goods which are profitable to produce will be valued in themselves by the producers. It should also be clear that, in most normal circumstances, profits arising from production will be a much more significant component in entrepreneurs' cost-benefit calculations than private consumption benefits with respect to the goods they produce. This is quite simply because the maximum potential production surplus is the total consumption surplus of every other member of the group. Only when entrepreneurs value the good much more highly than other group members is this evaluation likely to outweigh the potential profit available from supplying the good to the group. And only in these circumstances will the consumption component of their calculations outweigh the production component.

The foregoing suggests that, other things being equal, two factors will affect the relative weight which entrepreneurs attach to their private consumption preferences when formulating public goods packages. Firstly, it is clear that the relative weight of these consumption preferences will decline with the increasing size of the group. The larger the group, the greater the aggregate consumption surplus of every other member of the group, although the entrepreneurs' own consumption surplus remains unchanged. Secondly, increasing the intensity of competition faced by entrepreneurs will reduce the size of their production surplus, while leaving their consumption surplus unaffected. Thus, other things being equal, increased competition will increase the weight given by entrepreneurs to consumption preferences, although in all but the smallest groups this weight may still be very small. As the incentives for collusion, and hence the potential production surplus, increase, the relative weight of the personal preferences of entrepreneurs in the formulation of the public goods package will decline.

One additional factor will affect the importance of entrepreneurs' preferences in their decision-making. This is the amount of information they have about the preferences, and hence the consumption surpluses, of the rest of the group. In an extreme case, when entrepreneurs have absolutely no information about the preferences of the rest of the group, *any* public goods package is likely to be, for all they know, as profitable as any other. In these circumstances, personal public goods preferences will tip the balance, since the expected production surplus of every public goods package is identical. This situation is likely to confront both inexperienced entrepreneurs and entrepreneurs facing totally new issues, on which the preferences of their clientele are unknown. In these circumstances, the personal preferences of entrepreneurs are likely to determine their policy packages.

In normal circumstances, however, the consumption component of the entrepreneurs' calculations is likely to be outweighed by the production surplus. Consumption preferences will influence the policies put forward if the group is small enough, if competition is intense enough, or if information about the preferences of the group is bad enough, to produce relatively small expected differences between the production surplus associated with various alternative public goods packages. If these conditions are not fulfilled, the consumption preferences of entrepreneurs will only affect highly marginal specific calculations, and entrepreneurs will be mainly concerned with producing public goods packages at a profit, without concern for their own preferences.

POLITICAL PARTIES

Public entrepreneurs competing to produce public goods and thereby realize a surplus will have incentives to band themselves together into coalitions. Such coalitions of entrepreneurs will enable members to tender for very large public goods contracts beyond the scope of any individual entrepreneur, to gain strategic advantages over competitors, and to increase some of the benefits which can arise from collusion between otherwise competing individuals.

It is likely that, for all but the smallest groups, the scale of entrepreneurial activity involved in raising revenue for, and organizing the production of, public goods will be beyond the scope of a single individual. We have just seen that all contracts for the production of valued goods which are not susceptible to the exclusion of recalcitrant consumers will be awarded in a bundle, for a fixed term, to a single entrepreneur who is granted an effective monopoly. It will not be feasible for members of the group to split this bundle of contracts up and award components to separate entrepreneurs, since each entrepreneur would have an incentive to indulge in the competitive use of sanctions, imposing unnecessary costs on the group. Thus, public goods contracts will usually be very large. They may well need a team of entrepreneurs to finance the required scale of production. Furthermore, a single entrepreneur may not control the range of resources necessary to enable the production of the range of public goods desired by the group. A consortium of entrepreneurs with different skills and resources will be able to realize efficiency gains arising from the division of labour and responsibility between them, and hence be able to offer the group more competitive public goods contracts. Once one group of entrepreneurs has formed this type of consortium, it will almost certainly be necessary for rivals to do the same thing, if they are to offer competitive tenders to the group.

We have already seen that rival entrepreneurs will have an incentive to collude. This is because, by restricting competition, they can retain a higher level of surplus from public goods provision. We have also seen that the public goods contract will be awarded by the sub-group which controls a majority of coercive resources in the system. Entrepreneurs will thus appeal to such groups when offering public goods contracts. In the absence of perfect information about the resources and preferences of each member of the population, a number of sub-groups sharing common interests can potentially control a majority of the coercive resources. These may become 'target groups' for rival entrepreneurs, with different entrepreneurs offering contracts which are attractive to different groups. Each will hope that the group which favours the contract that they have on offer will turn out to control a majority of the coercive resources. This will mean that entrepreneurs appealing to completely different sub-groups of the population will not be in serious competition with one another, since a given public goods contract would have to decline considerably in its attractiveness before members of the target group at which it was aimed preferred an alternative contract, designed to appeal to a quite different target group. Competition between entrepreneurs with different target groups will thus be rather slack, and the incentives for them to collude will be correspondingly reduced. The extreme case of this occurs when two target groups have mutually exclusive preferences. Entrepreneurs trying to do business with the respective groups are not in competition with each other at all, since members of one group will never support policies designed to realize the preferences of the other group. Each entrepreneur will be in an effective monopoly position.[12]

Entrepreneurs appealing to the same target group will have much higher incentives to collude, for all the reasons discussed in the preceding argument. One effective method of collusion will be to transform a set of rival enterprises into a monopolistic joint venture. This will solve the day-to-day problems of allocating resources and side-payments, as well as avoiding potential disapproval from the group, which might be generated by the rather obvious alternative forms of restrictive practice. The incentives for collusion between rival entrepreneurs with the same target group will thus add to the incentives which already exist for them to combine into some form of consortium. This consortium would offer a single package to a given target group.

A further strategic advantage can often be gained by entrepreneurs who join forces. In a diverse population, it is quite possible that there will be a series of target groups, each with an entrepreneur offering them a different public goods package, but none of which controls a majority of coercive resources. It will be necessary for entrepreneurs serving different target groups to join forces in order to put together a package appealing to a target group which does control a majority of coercive resources. These coalitions of entrepreneurs may be temporary or permanent. In this system of shifting coalitions, a relatively large permanent unit can enjoy a strong bargaining position.

Entrepreneurs forming themselves into coalitions will need to agree upon how to divide up the surplus extracted by the coalition. Bargaining over the allocation of the surplus may well involve the use of threats. Entrepreneurs will be able to threaten the members of any given coalition that, if they are not adequately remunerated for their membership, they will form a coalition with rival entrepreneurs. Assuming for the moment that all other things are equal, so that all coalitions may potentially extract the same level of surplus from public goods provision, then the bargaining power of a particular entrepreneur or consortium will be directly related to the number of alternative winning coalitions which can be joined. These threats will obviously be empty if, after leaving the threatened coalition, it is still winning. Coalition members are thus unlikely to receive much surplus from those coalitions of which they are not essential members. Similarly, threatening to join a coalition of which the author of the threat is not an essential member will not cut much ice. Thus, entrepreneurs may threaten coalitions of which they are essential members with the possibility that they will join rival coalitions of which they are also essential members, and from which they may therefore reasonably expect to receive a share of the surplus. The bargaining power of entrepreneurs will thus be related to the number of winning coalitions of which they are essential members.

Consider, then, a collection of individual politicians, or evenly matched consortia, each competing with the others for resources. If two individuals or consortia combine, they may often more than double the number of winning coalitions of which they are essential members. The most obvious example of this occurs when three equally supported consortia confront each other. No single consortium controls a majority of coercive resources, but any two do between them. The three are evenly matched, and control one third of the bargaining power each. If any two are in coalition with one another, each member can threaten the other with the possibility of going into coalition with the third consortium. Any two who combine to form a single, indivisible unit can, however, guarantee complete control of the situation. They control all of the bargaining power, because the third consortium has nothing to threaten; it is an essential member of no winning coalition. The two combining groups between them control two thirds of the bargaining power before their union; after it they control all of the bargaining power.[13]

It is not, however, necessary for entrepreneurs to combine into units which are winning, before they can realize gains from combination. Bargaining power can often be increased by forming a unit which still does not control a majority of the coercive resources. For example, if there are five entrepreneurs, appealing to groups which have equal quantities of coercive resources, each entrepreneur will have one fifth of the total bargaining power. If two of these entrepreneurs combine to form a single, indivisible, unit, controlling double the coercive resources of each of the others, their combined bargaining power is more than doubled. There are now twenty-four possible ways of putting together a winning coalition of entrepreneurs, and the new, larger, consortium is essential to half of these.[14] By combining, the two entrepreneurs have increased their aggregate bargaining power from two fifths to one half of the total, with a commensurate increase in their expectations. This gain in power is at the expense of the others who have not combined. These will, in turn, have incentives to look for other combinations which counteract this. If the weight of an individual or consortium is related to the proportion of coercive resources controlled, then, given any configuration of weights, there is almost always at least one pair of actors who can combine and thereby increase their aggregate bargaining power. (While I have not seen a formal proof of this proposition, I have yet to come across a configuration of weights which contradicts it.)[15] The enhanced bargaining power of larger, indivisible, consortia of entrepreneurs will thus provide a further incentive for these entrepreneurs to combine. The search for opportunities to extract resources from rivals, when cooperation is necessary in order to be able to offer viable public goods contracts, will encourage entrepreneurs to fuse into larger and larger units.

Public entrepreneurs will thus have at least three types of incentive to form consortia. They need to be able to control sufficient skills and resources to be able to submit realistic tenders for public goods contracts to large groups. They will want to collude to restrict competition if they are competing for the loyalty of the same target group. And they will want to gain the bargaining advantages produced by combination. Taken together, these incentives suggest not only that such consortia will form, but also that they will contain entrepreneurs appealing to broadly similar target groups.

4 The Logic of Voting

Public entrepreneurs form coalitions in order to compete more effectively for public goods contracts, and to increase the surplus available if they succeed in winning these contracts. These coalitions will compete with each other for the approval of a group within the population which controls a majority of the coercive resources, since such a group can award a contract which cannot be effectively challenged by any other group. The more equal distribution of coercive resources in the population, the less information about this distribution, and the more diverse the interests of the population, then the more likely it is that a group which controls a majority of the coercive resources will also contain a majority of the population. If these conditions are fulfilled, therefore, any contract which is preferred to any other by a majority of the population is likely to be stable. The award of this contract may, in these circumstances, be conducted by a ballot of the population, the contract being granted to the coalition or coalitions of entrepreneurs putting forward a contract which secures majority approval. The rest of this chapter concerns the competition which is likely to take place when these conditions are fulfilled. Public entrepreneurs will henceforth be described as 'politicians', coalitions of entrepreneurs will be described as 'parties', the rest of the group as 'voters' and the ballot as an 'election'.

Throughout this discussion it must be remembered that we have deduced *instrumental* motivations for participation by politicians in competition for public goods contracts. These instrumental motivations will largely arise from the production surplus available from producing public goods at a profit, although the politicians' consumption surplus may influence their programmes when the group is small, competition intense, or information very bad. We have excluded consideration of any intrinsic satisfactions accruing to politicians as a result of competition *per se*, since these would be socially conditioned and therefore destroy the fundamental character of the explanation.

Party competition is one of the best known subjects of the rational choice literature which is characterized by its deference to the seminal contribution made by Anthony Downs in *An Economic Theory of Democracy*.[1] These writings are concerned with the interaction between, on the one hand, a group of voters, each of whom is trying to maximize personal well-being, and, on the other hand, a group of politicians, each of whom is trying to maximize his chances of getting into power. In Downs's original formulation, the distinctions between the different types of motivation for participating in politics are rather blurred. Politicians are seen as being motivated by the desire to maximize votes above all else. This is presented as a parsimonious summary of all their various other objectives, which include:

> ... the desire for power, prestige, and income and ... the love of conflict ... However they can obtain none of these desiderata except the last unless their party is elected to office. Therefore we do not distort the motives of party members by saying that their primary objective is to be elected.[2]

A politician is thus a rather different creature from an ordinary voter, who 'casts his vote for the party who will provide him with more benefits than any other'.[3] In other words, while everyone wants to maximize personal well-being, politicians are also motivated by the desire for power and prestige. Our discussion of the entrepreneurial role of politicians has shown that, if everyone wants to maximize surplus, and surplus can be realized by producing public goods at a profit, politicians will *instrumentally* value power to the extent that it helps them further this objective. The desire of politicians to maximize power and their desire to maximize votes arise from their desire to maximize the production surplus arising from public goods provision. Vote-maximizing activity which is engaged in for reasons other than the instrumental realization of fundamental intrinsic goals, for example competing for the love of competition, must be regarded as irrational. Conversely, we must consider as rational activity anything which increases entrepreneurial surplus, even if it has no effect on voting strength.

With this *caveat*, there is no need for more than the very briefest rehearsal of Downs's argument, which has been extensively discussed elsewhere.[4] Parties are assumed to be homogeneous groups of politicians, which function as single, unitary, actors. They formulate ideologies, or packages of policies, to reduce the cost to voters of collecting and evaluating the vast amount of information necessary to make an optimal voting-decision. Ideologies also provide parties with an aura of stability and consistency which, they hope, will increase voters' evaluations of their competence and good faith. Parties' policies can be arranged along a single ideological dimension, which more or less corresponds to the familiar left–right dimension of socio-economic policy. Individual voters have a set of policy preferences, which can be aggregated in such a way that they will most prefer a policy package which occupies a particular point on this ideological dimension. Parties compete with each other by modifying their policies and effectively shifting their position on the ideological spectrum. Voters vote for the party which occupies the position closest to their most preferred position. The objective of a party strategist is to set party policy at a position on the ideological spectrum which maximizes the number of voters who prefer that policy to the policy put forward by any other party.

Considerable theoretical development has taken place in this general field, throughout all of which one essential feature has been preserved. Each rational choice theory of party competition has been based on the assumption that people *vote rationally* and predictably. Each approach makes specific assumptions about the preferences of the electorate. Each is based on these assumptions and the deduction that rational voters will, consciously or unconsciously, balance the various programmes of the competing parties, and vote instrumentally for the one which offers them most. The rational voter has become the corner-stone of rational choice theories of party competition; theories of voting behaviour and party competition are inextricably intertwined.

TO VOTE OR NOT TO VOTE?

For the reasons outlined in the preceding paragraph, we need to have a very clear idea of why people vote. The precise nature of the assumptions made about the electorate is subject to considerable variation between authors, however. These need further consideration in the light of the fact that we have at this stage made only the most general of assumptions about voters' preferences. Rationality has been assumed to be utility-maximization, and the set of goals from which voters might derive utility has been completely unconstrained. The problem is that, if voters are liable to want absolutely anything, this will not provide politicians with much information upon which to base their party policy. Further assumptions are necessary, if statements about the electorate are to be used as a basis for a theory of party competition. The need to constrain the set of goals desired by voters is made particularly acute in the context of the 'calculus of voting' problem, which has concerned most authors in this general field.[5]

If the voters are rational and if voting involves some cost (in the form of information-gathering, decision-taking, shoe leather, and general mental distress during election campaigns), then a real benefit must accrue from the act of voting. Despite this, the influence that a particular voter wields over the decision-making process is likely to be extremely small. In all but the smallest of electorates, the voter is likely to have an almost infinitesimal effect on the eventual public goods package that is produced. The difference between the various packages on offer may be quite large, but it is likely that each voter, considering the tiny chance of actually bringing about even a large change in policy, will not expect a worthwhile return on the investment. This expectation is unlikely to be balanced by any realistic level of voting costs. The low expectations associated with voting are the crux of the calculus of voting problem; the consequences of voting are so unlikely to offset the costs that it would not seem to be rational to vote at all. If voters incur these costs regardless, we must regard them as irrational. Our ability to solve this problem determines our ability to use assumptions about voter rationality to explain their behaviour in voting. If we cannot do this, we cannot use these assumptions to *deduce* a rational choice theory of party competition.

A number of solutions to the problem of why people vote at all have been suggested, the first of which was expounded by Downs himself. Downs attempted to deduce real benefits for the individual consequent upon the act of voting by arguing that, if no one voted, democracy would collapse.[6] In our terms, the argument can be restated thus. If no one voted, no threat would be posed to the incumbent, who would therefore have no incentive to provide public goods at other than the most minimal level necessary to stop clients tearing up their contracts. The provision of public goods would therefore be extremely sub-optimal. Downs argues that, if this were to happen, then everyone would suffer, including non-voters. He claims that voters incur the costs of voting in order to insure themselves against the very high costs they would face if competition were to collapse:

> ... if voting costs exist, pursuit of short-run rationality can conceivably cause democracy to break down. However improbable this outcome may seem, it is so disastrous that every citizen is willing to bear at least some cost in order to insure himself against it. The more probable it appears, the more cost he is willing to bear.[7]

Our discussion of the role of competition between entrepreneurs over the provision of public goods has already shown that this argument is logically incoherent. Competition is a public good and, as such, susceptible to free-riding. Just as voters will not contribute towards the costs of opponents of the incumbent in exchange for the provision of the public good of opposition, they will not voluntarily incur voting costs to further the same objective. Voters can enjoy the benefits of competition between entrepreneurs, whether or not they contribute to this by voting. It is inconceivable that the vote of any individual is going to make the difference between the collapse of competition or not. Thus, voting does not yield any directly consequential increase in utility income, and people will not vote to insure themselves against the collapse of 'democracy'. The reason is precisely that each voter cannot insure *himself* or *herself*, but can insure the *whole group*, against the collapse of competition, because competition is a public good. It will always be rational for any individual voter to stay in bed, and let the rest insure society against collapse. The fact that, if everyone thinks like this, society will indeed collapse, makes no difference.

Since competition between politicians is a public good, and since one of the factors of production of this good is the behaviour of the electorate, we might wish to explore further the means by which competition may be provided. Anarchistic methods of provision may be suitable, since competition is, *in extremis*, an all-or-nothing good produced by behaviour modification which does not involve the long-term commitment of resources. If a group of voters is small enough that anarchistic arrangements are likely to work, a conditional agreement along the lines 'we will all vote as long as we all vote' might emerge. If unanimous participation was not necessary for the provision of competition, some voters would take free rides, but, once the minimum level of voting necessary to ensure continued competition had been reached, each voter still voting would have a positive incentive to continue to do so. Competition would be produced, although it would continually be on the brink of collapse. Alternatively, an entrepreneur could offer, as part of a public goods package, a proposal to apply sanctions to all non-voters. If this was accepted, voting would be made compulsory, and since this measure would ensure the public good of competition, it would be quite rational for each voter to accept – though not to vote for – a package containing this proposal. Short of compulsion, however, it is unlikely that voters in large electorates will regard the costs of making up their minds and turning out to vote as offset by any directly consequential benefits in terms of increased competition.

A quite different approach is adopted by Riker and Ordeshook in their writings on the calculus of voting. They reject Downs's solution, and instead rely upon a number of assumed 'positive components' in the voters' cost-benefit calculation. Voters are assumed to derive positive satisfactions from complying with the ethic of voting, affirming allegiance to the political system, affirming partisan preference, affirming efficacy in the political system and from going to the polls (!).[8] These positive components are neither deduced nor interpreted in instrumental terms by Riker and Ordeshook, but introduced as social assumptions in their own right. They therefore completely undermine the fundamental character of any explanation of voting. The satisfaction derived from going to the polls' is the most blatant example of this, since, if it is accepted, we explain the political act of voting simply by saying that people vote because they want to. The assumed satisfactions arising from affirming efficacy in the political system and affirming allegiance to the political system have very much the same effect. An assumed satisfaction derived by voters from affirming a partisan preference has equally damaging consequences for a rational theory of party competition, leaving aside the fact that it is an *a priori*, yet social, assumption. If people enjoy voting for a political party *in general*, it is difficult to reasonably exclude the possibility that they enjoy in particular the act of voting for a specific political party. In other words, our theory of party competition would contain the proposition not only that people vote because they want to, but also that they vote for the party of their choice because they want to do this as well. This in itself would be completely empty theory, quite apart from failing to provide a fundamental potential explanation of anything. It would of course, be possible to attempt to establish empirically the various correlates of particular propensities to turn out and to vote for particular parties, but in so doing we would have stepped completely outside any process of deductive explanation. If such correlates were established, they might form the basis of an explanation of voting, but the logic of the theory would be inductive rather than deductive, and therefore outside the rational choice paradigm. This type of theoretical development does, of course, form the basis of quite a different, sociological, account of voting, the party-identification theories of the Michigan School.[9]

The final positive component alluded to by Riker and Ordeshook is the 'satisfaction of complying with the ethic of voting'. While they do not provide an instrumental justification for the existence of an 'ethic of voting' in a particular group, such a justification could possibly be produced, in terms of an argument rather similar to the one used above to explore the rationality of voting in order to produce the public good of competition. We saw that although voters would not make voluntary contributions towards the costs of providing the public good of opposition, they may well be aware that, if no one votes, this public good will not be produced, competition will collapse and they will all be worse off. One possible solution was for them to come to a conditional agreement that they would each vote as long as they all voted, while another was to accept some form of compulsion. A hybrid of these two alternatives would be to develop some form of semi-institutionalized norm or 'ethic' of voting. This ethic would be enforced on the basis of informal social sanctions. People could be nasty to non-voters, refuse to cooperate with them over other matters, and so on. In this way, non-voters might incur real private disadvantages as a direct consequence of their decision not to bother participating in elections. A very important precondition for this ethic to be effective, of course, is for non-voters to be identified. If voting is secret, or if it is otherwise impossible to identify non-voters, the ethic of voting will not influence voters one little bit. This is because the satisfaction of complying is more realistically viewed as an avoidance of the informal sanctions provoked by not complying. Thus, in systems where voting is public and non-voters can be identified, an ethic of voting might conceivably arise which provides individuals with sufficient incentive for them to turn out and vote. If voting is a private activity, this cannot provide a solution to the calculus of voting problem.

Thus Riker and Ordeshook's positive components to the voting decision either undermine the fundamental character of the explanation of voting, and cannot be used as the basis of a rational theory of party competition, or they depend on an assumption of public voting and easily identifiable recalcitrance. If this condition cannot be satisfied, none of their positive components is of any help.

A third possible solution to the calculus of voting problem is to argue that voting costs are very small. If this is the case, then even a tiny probability of influencing the result may offset any costs incurred in attempting to do so. Some voters will never find it worthwhile, given their expectations, either because their subjective estimate of the probability of influencing the result is very small, or because the benefits they expect from actually succeeding in having an effect are not worth the costs. Other voters may be more optimistic about their efficacy, or value the benefits of succeeding more highly. Thus, other things being equal, those perceiving little difference between the alternative public goods packages on offer would be less likely to turn out and vote than those who perceive a larger difference. This deduction could of course be tested empirically. As well as perceiving different benefits consequent upon the act of voting, different individuals are likely to face different voting costs in different situations. A further series of propositions can be deduced from this and tested empirically. Voting costs will include both the cost of turning out and voting and the cost of deciding how to vote. We have already seen that Downs presents the development of party ideologies as one method which parties have of reducing their clients' voting costs, by making their decision more straightforward. The more complex and incomprehensible the decisions faced by voters, the less likely they are to bother voting. As well as helping voters with their decision costs, parties can also try to reduce the cost of turning out, by providing transport to the polling-booth and so on. Parties have an incentive to do this only for those individuals who they anticipate will actually vote for them, of course, and we will return to this point in the discussion of party competition proper. Other exogenous factors affect voters' costs. These include the weather, the distance travelled to the polling-point, the convenience of the voting period and so on. As these costs increase, turn-out should decrease. If turn-out is volatile and highly susceptible to these relatively minor costs, this would provide evidence in support of the assumption that voting costs are small and the voter's decision to turn out relatively marginal. One possible reason why voting costs are lower than might superficially be thought to be the case arises from satisficing by voters. If voters perceive little difference between alternative ways of voting (taking into account the likelihood of influencing the result and the likely benefits of succeeding), then they will not voluntarily incur decision costs, and may reduce their voting costs to those actually involved in the physical act of voting itself. If these fixed costs are outweighed by the benefits, then voting will be rational although the direction of the vote will be determined by the information the voter has already, or picks up for nothing. We will return to the implications of this later.

Each of these interpretations of the rationality of turning out to vote has implicitly assumed a set of voters' goals which is more restricted than the one we assumed in the first chapter. These constraints are best illustrated in comparison with the final account of the calculus of voting which we will consider. This is advanced by David Robertson in *A Theory of Party Competition*. Robertson insists on retaining a completely unconstrained definition of rationality. He argues that, since a rational individual is anyone who can produce an instrumental justification for his actions, almost anything, including voting, can be explained as rational behaviour, if it is carried out in pursuit of some goal or other. He cites the example, first used by Downs, of the voter's wife. The voter votes for B, rather than A, despite the fact that he prefers A to B.[10] He might equally vote when he would prefer not to vote. When challenged, the voter produces the explanation that his wife would give him a really bad time if she were to discover that he had stayed at home, or gone to the pub. If the desire to please his wife is the deciding factor in this person's voting calculation, then his action can indeed be seen as rational and instrumental in terms of the very broad definition of the set of possible goals which we have used so far. It should also be clear, however, that if this is as far as we are prepared to go, then it is as far as we *can* go. We certainly cannot go on to construct a theory of party competition based on deductions from voter rationality. In this context, a rational voter is liable to do almost anything. Parties could not behave rationally on the basis of information like that. In other words, if we retain the broad definition of rationality, it is almost impossible to deduce anything from voting behaviour.

The alternative, implicitly adopted by the other interpretations of voting we have considered, is to make further assumptions about the set of goals preferred by the electorate. Specifically they assume that while, in the most general terms, a rational voter might have any goal at all, the voters considered by theories of party competition possess a subset of the universe of all possible goals, containing all of those goals which concern the enhancement of the economic well-being of the individual concerned. Thus, actions are preferred which increase economic well-being, and actions are avoided which yield net opportunity costs in terms of economic well-being. Downs, for example, devotes almost his entire analysis to the pursuit by voters of socio-economic objectives. Most other authors have followed in his footsteps, although some have added further subsets of goals containing, for example, linguisitic, ethnic or religious aspirations. Constraining the set of possible goals in this way has the effect of making an important, restrictive, assumption about the nature of the electorate. It is this assumption which forms the basis of most rational choice theories of party competition, since it provides a basis for rational action by parties. The set of goals need not, of course, be constrained by considering only economic objectives; any other generalizable constraints would do the trick, even the assumption that voters act to please their wives, if we knew what the wives wanted. The assumption that voters pursue socio-economic goals is by far and away the most common one made, implicitly or explicitly, by authors of rational choice theories of party competition. The consequence of this is that we must be able to explain the act of turning out and voting in terms of the restricted set of voters' goals that we are really using.

Thus the calculus of voting problem can be solved in two ways, assuming that the electorate is sufficiently large for non-voting to be undetectable, and assuming that voting is not compulsory. We can either retain a completely unconstrained definition of rationality, allowing voters to possess all types of intrinsically and instrumentally valued goals. In this case we solve the calculus of voting problem 'at a stroke'. We can imagine any number of motivations which might induce people to vote, even after excluding those which are instrumentally valued yet socially conditioned. Instead, we are left with a 'theory of party competition problem', since we do not have a set of assumptions which form the basis of such a theory. On the other hand, we can restrict the set of goals which we assume voters to possess, in which case we do have a 'calculus of voting' problem. The only coherent method of solving this for large electorates is to make the assumption that voting costs are very low. Further empirical substantiation of this proposition would therefore seem to be a high priority. This particular explanation of voting becomes the cornerstone of a rational choice theory of party competition based upon assumptions about the generalizable goals of voters.

If voting costs are low, and the voter's decision to turn out is marginal, then the traditional Downsian account of voting behaviour and party competition can be made to cohere. Each elector votes for the party which looks most likely to provide the highest utility income, taking into account the various public goods packages on offer and the likelihood that each of these will bear fruit. This in turn involves an evaluation of both the feasibility of the packages themselves and the capacity of the parties offering them to put them into practice. If these packages are arrayed along an ideological spectrum, voters choose the party whose policy package lies closest on the spectrum to their own preferred policies. Elections are decided on the basis of the ideological preferences in the electorate, together with each voter's evaluation of the feasibility of the policies and the plausibility of the parties.

DECIDING HOW TO VOTE

Assuming that the act of voting involves small costs to the voter, we have seen that people may or may not turn out, depending on the perceived costs and benefits involved. Many of the costs of voting will be determined by factors which lie outside the scope of the model. These include the weather, the distance of each voter from the polling-point, the inconvenience of the voting times, and so on. On the other hand, many of the potential benefits of voting will arise from the precise nature of competition between political parties. These benefits will depend crucially on differences between the various public goods packages on offer, given that the object of voting is to influence the probability that one or other of these packages will actually be put into practice. If all voters have the same preferences with respect to public goods, then the packages put forward by the various parties will be evaluated mainly in terms of the relative consumption surplus that each package makes available to the electorate. This will in turn have two principal components, reflecting the level of surplus retained by, and the efficiency or productivity of, the producer. In other words, if all voters have the same policy preferences, their decision will be made on the basis of their perceptions of the relative willingness and ability of politicians to turn a given level of revenue into various levels of public goods provision.

The level of surplus retained by politicians will in turn depend on the degree of competition in the system. We saw in the previous chapter that the less the diversity of preference in the electorate, the greater the incentive for politicians, or coalitions of politicians, to collude in order to reduce competition and raise the level of surplus that they can extract. Similarly, an incumbent who does not face a serious challenge from aspiring producers of public goods will be inclined to increase the level of surplus retained, either until such a challenge is provoked, or until the level of public goods provision is so low that voters tear up their contracts because the costs of public goods provided are less than the benefits. When there is no diversity of preference in the electorate, therefore, voters have an incentive to vote for opponents of the incumbent. This is either because a particular challenger seems likely to retain less surplus or because increasing support for the challenger increases the level of competition in the system, and hence encourages the incumbent to produce more public goods for a given volume of contributions, and to retain a smaller surplus. The increase in the level of competition produced by voting for a challenger is, of course, a public good, and will only be produced if the private benefits to each individual exceed the private costs. This is unlikely to be the case with respect to a single voter, but it does provide an incentive for voters to organize themselves into coalitions, if such a coalition can command sufficient support to materially affect the level of competition, or the result, of the election. Just as producers have an incentive to collude if, by so doing, they can raise the level of surplus they extract from consumers, so consumers have an incentive to collude to combat this process.

Collusion between voters will, of course, be more difficult to organize than collusion between producers, since there will usually be many more of them. However, relatively small groups of voters may materially affect their aggregate voting strength, if they can coordinate their activity. Since this collusion involves the modification of behaviour rather than the commitment of future resources, it is at least conceivable that the public goods produced by collusion between voters can be produced along anarchistic lines. Alternatively, a challenger may privately underwrite the costs of organizing voters in opposition to an incumbent, if this increases the chance of being able to take over profitable public goods contracts. The costs of such organization may well be rather small relative to the potential benefits both to the challenger and to the voters concerned. We will refer to this type of collusion between voters as pressure group activity. Even when there is no diversity in the preferences of the electorate, therefore, there are incentives for voters to form pressure groups in order to force incumbent politicians to retain lower levels of surplus for themselves. In these circumstances, it can conceivably become rational to vote in order to raise the level of competition in the system.

The relative attractiveness of various public goods packages to an electorate with no diversity of preference will also depend on the efficiency or productivity of the producer. Voters' evaluations of this will depend partly on their estimation of the intrinsic feasibility and coherence of the packages on offer, and partly on their estimation of the competence of the producer. When discussing an individual's own internal decision-making process in attempting to maximize utility, we argued that some sets of goals will contain elements (such as walking on water) which are intrinsically unrealizable, as well as subsets of elements (such as lying in bed all day and having a perfect physique) which will be intrinsically incompatible. Furthermore, given a particular limited supply of resources, many more examples of the short supply of goals will emerge. Voters will obviously evaluate the promises made by competing parties in the same terms. They will not believe politicians who promise to walk on water, or promise to simultaneously give them perfect bodies and allow them to lie in bed all day. Neither will they believe politicians who promise to raise very low levels of tax revenue, and provide in exchange very high levels of public goods. Voters will thus have *a priori* criteria at their disposal with which to evaluate the promises made to them by politicians. When a particular competitive system has been operating for some time, however, they will also be able to compare the promises made by politicians with their past practice. They will probably be less inclined to believe promises similar to those which have failed in the past. They will at least demand explanations of why, given that a particular package has previously failed, it should now succeed.

The other component of the efficiency of a particular package is the competence of the producer. Voters may make subjective estimates of this, based on all sorts of information. Particularly useful information will be available when the politician concerned is, or has been, an incumbent. Poor previous performance will reduce subjective estimates of competence, while good previous performance will enhance these estimates. This is likely to make an incumbent producing satisfactory levels of public goods appear more attractive than a challenger with no experience. Conversely, an inexperienced challenger may appear more attractive than an unsatisfactory incumbent.

The efficiency of producers of public goods will also be affected by the level of competition in the system. This is the concern of the main part of Albert Hirschman's discussion of the production of public goods in *Exit, Voice and Loyalty*.[11] Hirschman argues that, when competition is slack, the level of public goods provision may decline as a result of the deteriorating efficiency of the producers, even without any consequential increase in the level of surplus they retain. Since taut competition provides at least one test of efficiency, slack competition undermines at least one of the feedback mechanisms available to producers to enable them to assess their performance. Increasing the level of competition in the system may therefore increase the level of public goods provision, by increasing the efficiency of producers as well as by reducing the level of retained surplus. Once more, while an individual voter is unlikely to be able to increase the level of competition as a result of his or her own activity, we see further incentives for voters to collude in pressure groups. Such collusion, if it is organized at all, may be organized along the lines discussed above, either as a result of anarchistic agreements, or of being financed privately by challengers.

So far we have been assuming that every voter in the electorate has the same set of preferences with respect of public goods provision. This assumption is obviously extremely restrictive. If we allow for a diversity of preferences in the electorate, then the precise nature of the various public goods packages on offer will become a significant component of the decision made by each voter. We saw in the previous chapter that incentives for politicians to collude are reduced by the existence of diverse preferences in the electorate, since different coalitions of politicians may well address themselves to different target groups. When different voters prefer different mixes of public goods, the same public goods package will give each of them a different utility income. As a consequence, the cost-benefit calculations associated with voting become more complex.

For voters with fixed small voting costs, the attractiveness of turning out to vote will depend on the difference between the utility income produced by their most favoured public goods package and that produced by their second choice, assuming that they have no information about the likely outcome of the election. The larger the gap between the policy packages representing first and second choices, the more attractive voting becomes, for a given cost. If the two packages are very similar, voting would make little difference, even if it was effective in changing the outcome of the election. For a given voting cost, two policy packages can become sufficiently similar for it not to be worthwhile expending resources on voting, or sufficiently different to make voting worthwhile. Turn-out is thus likely to decrease, other things being equal, as the policy packages on offer become more similar.

Since we are concerned with the *perceived* differences between policy packages, it is furthermore possible to assume that the perceived difference between two alternatives decreases as those alternatives become less attractive. In other words, we could assume that a given difference between two policies seems much larger to those who rather like the policies than it does to those who detest them. This is of course an *ad hoc* assumption, but it is at least fundamental and asocial in character, and therefore does not violate the principles of our methodology. The consequence of this assumption is that, if the diverse preferences of the electorate are represented along some sort of ideological spectrum as Downs suggests, then voters will be less inclined to turn out and vote, the further they are on the spectrum from the closest policy packages on offer. One consequence of this would be that voters at the furthest extremes of the policy spectrum would be unlikely to turn out and vote, since it is unlikely that any politician would perceive any electoral advantage in offering policies close to those that these voters prefer. (This is unless, of course, the majority of voters were located at the extremes of the policy spectrum.) Whatever happens, however, the less the gap between the various policy packages on offer, the less attractive voting will be.

If voters are able to make some estimate of the likely outcome of the election, their voting decisions become still more complex. This is because there is no incentive to turn out and vote if they have no hope of influencing the result, bearing in mind that one component of this result will be the level of competition in the system. If a voter is not involved in collusion with others in order to raise the level of competition in the system, then any estimate of the likelihood of influencing the result will depend not only on the number of other voters, but also on the precise ways in which those others are likely to cast their ballot. If the rest of the electorate is likely to behave in such a way as to render the alternatives preferred by a given voter either highly likely or highly unlikely to prevail, that voter will judge that his or her action will not make any difference. Voters who prefer unpopular policy packages, or prefer very popular packages, are likely to anticipate a low return on their investment in voting costs. Other things being equal, these voters are therefore less likely to bother to turn out than those who prefer policies which may or may not prevail. Assuming fixed small voting costs, therefore, voters are less likely to turn out if they prefer popular or unpopular policies, or if they think the policies on offer are rather similar. As we saw in the previous chapter, voters may economize on their voting costs by expending little or no resources in making the optimum decision. This form of satisficing may still result in voting, but in much less calculated voting than would otherwise be the case. In this case, the factors which influence the direction of the vote will obviously be more variable and unpredictable than if voters simply vote for the policy which makes them best off. Voters may vote in the same way as others in the same situation, as their parents, or on the basis of any number of cues and stimuli. The systematic analysis of these predispositions is, of course, a matter of empirical research.[12] For the purpose of this discussion, however, it must be remembered that the outcome of all this is a substitute for maximizing behaviour when the stakes are seen to be low, and when the probability of influencing the result is low. Furthermore, it should never dictate a course of action which runs counter to perceived self-interest. When the stakes or the probabilities are higher, then rational voting should more closely approximate to utility-maximization. We will consider the effect of this on party competition in the next chapter.

Diversity of preference in the electorate is likely to produce diversity in the public goods packages on offer. This raises the possibility that voters confronted with a choice of packages, none of which coincides with their own preferences, may consider the possibility of withholding their support for a particular politician, or even giving it to a rival, in order to try to force the politician to put forward a package which more closely corresponds with their preferences. Such a threat is obviously only effective if it is communicated to the politician concerned, and is very unlikely to be heeded if it is made by a single individual. This possibility does, however, provide another incentive for collusion between voters. If a group of voters share the same preferences, which are not reflected in the packages on offer, they can combine to make threats, collectively, which will be much more effective than those made as individuals. They could threaten to withhold their combined support, unless changes are made in the policies on offer by a particular entrepreneur. While this threat might induce a politician to modify the policies on offer, we need to explain how this type of collective action on the part of the voters might come to pass. This problem is more acute than the one faced when trying to explain pressure group activity conducted in order to raise the level of competition, since, by definition, there will be no challenging politician available who will have an interest in underwriting any collusion costs. If such a politician existed, he or she could put forward the appropriate policies and obviate the need for voter collusion. The necessity for collusion between voters arises because there are no politicians who are prepared to modify their policies in this manner.

If collective action by voters sharing similar preferences cannot be organized along anarchistic lines, presumably because the group is too large, there is one other potential source of support. This depends upon the assumption that different packages of public goods will involve different suppliers of factors of production. In these circumstances, those suppliers of factors of production who would benefit from a change in policy would have an incentive to underwrite the costs of a voter cartel aimed at producing the appropriate policy change. Thus if, for example, a particular sub-goup of voters wanted an increase in the level of construction of public buildings, then the suppliers of building materials would have an incentive to underwrite any of the costs of organizing a pressure group of voters to bring this about. The interaction between the private goods market and the public goods market may be sufficient to support the existence of pressure groups whose objectives include the modification of public policy. This possibility arises for the same reasons that private suppliers may fund a rival entrepreneur. The costs of organizing the collective action by voters may be small compared to the private benefits the suppliers may receive, if that collective action is successful and different public goods packages are produced.

To sum up, if voting costs are small, voters will have a number of incentives to vote and to collude with other voters in pressure groups. The general level of competition in the system will be affected by the number of people voting. This is a public good, but may be produced by coalitions of voters either organized anarchistically, or financed by a challenger. This competition will affect the level of surplus retained by politicians and their productive efficiency. Voters will be able to assess the efficiency of politicians, both in terms of intrinsic *a priori* criteria and in terms of past performance. When diversity of preference exists in the electorate, the gap between the various public goods packages on offer will affect each voter's propensity to turn out: the wider the gap, the more likely each is to consider the costs of voting worthwhile. Taking into account the likely result of the election, voters who prefer either very popular or very unpopular packages of public goods are less likely to turn out, because they are less likely to affect the result. Groups of voters preferring similar packages, which are not on offer, may try and collude to force a politician to offer the package they want. The costs of this collusion may be underwritten by the suppliers of factors of production who benefit from the relevant change in policy.

BEYOND ECONOMIC GOALS

So far, in considering the constraints on the set of voters' goals necessary to produce assumptions which form the basis of a theory of party competition, we have taken account only of socio-economic aspirations. This is the solution adopted by Downs himself, and by many of his followers, but some subsequent authors have been more ambitious and added other, independent, dimensions of party and voter ideology. These additional dimensions represent religious, ethnic, linguistic and rural–urban cleavages, and so on.[13] Since we were forced to constrain the set of voters' goals to enable us to simultaneously solve the calculus of voting problem and produce a theory of party competition, it should be clear that these extensions of the scope of ideology are more than 'mere' generalizations. They have fundamental implications for the whole approach. If we add a linguistic dimension to our representation of electoral behaviour, we are not simply refining it to make it more realistic; we are redefining the subset of goals which we assume voters to pursue.

On one hand, many additional sets of goals which we might wish to assume may be valued for instrumental reasons. For example, speaking another language, or not speaking it, may involve the actual expenditure of resources, as well as costs in terms of lost opportunities. Thus, a set of linguistic aspirations in the electorate may have an entirely economic rationale. A public goods package which changed the official language of the group might be favoured or detested entirely because of its economic implications for those concerned. Alternatively, a rural–urban conflict might be motivated by entirely mercenary considerations, with voters living in the country preferring the production of public goods which helped the rural population, and voters living in cities preferring those which helped city folk. In each case, the addition of a new set of instrumental goals would not involve any major reconsideration of the calculus of voting problem or the theory of party competition problem, since the underlying dynamic in the system would still be the maximization of economic well-being. The new categories of goals could all be subsumed within the narrow, economic definition of voter rationality. Despite this, it may well be necessary to introduce further ideological dimensions into our model, if we wish to plausibly represent the packages on offer from politicians, and the preferences of the electorate, in spatial terms. The fact that instrumentally valued goals can be reduced to economic well-being does not mean that they can all be represented on a single dimension of ideology. It is still possible to independently prefer, for example, high or low levels of rural expenditure and high or low levels of welfare expenditure. New sets of instrumentally valued goals may well complicate any spatial representation of party competition.

The addition of new sets of goals which are intrinsically valued, however, does force us to reconsider our assumptions. By definition, new types of intrinsically valued goals cannot be described entirely in terms of economic well-being. We have of course stated that no socially determined goals may be intrinsically valued, but we have not argued that the only possible intrinsically valued goals are economic. Linguistic aspirations, for example, *may* be simply motivated by economics, but may also be motivated by the aesthetic satisfactions that individuals derive from speaking their mother tongue. Similarly, religious aspirations may represent economic deprivation and discrimination of a certain type, but may also be related to the intrinsic satisfactions arising from the practice of a particular faith.

The problem created by importing new types of intrinsically

valued goal into our representation of voting behaviour is that we are forced to expand our narrow definition of rationality, the definition which solved the calculus of voting problem and the theory of party competition problem at the same time. Any expansion of the set of voters' goals must continue to be such that these problems do not reappear. This will mean that new sets of goals must be capable of definition according to relatively straightforward and generalizable criteria, so that the set of assumptions we are left with is a suitable basis for a theory of party competition. Language, religion and race are clearly satisfactory criteria in these terms, but there are many criteria which the theorist might be tempted to introduce which are not. These might include consideration of the personality of the candidates – unless it was possible to make sensible generalizations about this – and any number of other factors which might, in a perfect world, seem useful things to include if we are trying to explain how people vote.

5 The Logic of Party Competition

So far, we have painted a picture of politics which portrays political parties as coalitions of entrepreneurs, competing with each other to offer the public goods contract which receives the support of a majority of the electorate. Electors are assumed to be motivated by the desire to maximize their economic well-being; they therefore vote for the party which offers the public goods contract which seems most likely to do this. We also assume that there is in the electorate a diversity of preferences for various public goods packages. Politicians are concerned solely to get into office. They would prefer their party to be the exclusive incumbent but, failing this, want to belong to an incumbent coalition of parties. If members of a party anticipate entering into coalition with other parties, they will want to exert maximum bargaining strength in that coalition. In any case, the instrumental goals of politicians are best served by the maximization of the votes they receive at elections. Increasing the number of votes they receive increases both the chance that their party will gain majority support from the electorate, and the bargaining strength of the party if majority support is not achieved. Finally, it is assumed that the electorate is sufficiently large for the private *consumption* surplus of politicians with respect to public goods to be small, relative to the *production* surplus which can be achieved by implementing any particular public goods package. Politicians will therefore be concerned to maximize their production surplus, and will not allow their private consumption preferences to influence the public goods packages that they offer. In other words, we will assume for the moment that politicians will promise to deliver *anything*, regardless of their own preferences, if this is likely to maximize the number of votes received.[1]

TWO PARTIES

The most straightforward type of party competition is that between an incumbent and a single challenger, and we will consider this first, since it enables us to discuss, in simple terms, many of the important issues. In these circumstances, there will usually be a single public goods package which maximizes the support of a majority of the electorate, although we saw in Chapter 3 that there will be certain distributions of preferences which produce no single optimum package, and consequently yield cyclical majorities. Resurrecting the example used in Chapter 3, consider three groups, any two of which can control a majority, who rank three packages in the order, respectively: (defence, environment, health), (environment, health, defence) and (health, defence, environment). Two parties competing for majority support would be forced to continually change their policies, since there is no package which guarantees a majority with respect to both of the other two. The outcome would be indeterminate, and decided by chance factors. There are a number of ways in which we can constrain this indeterminate outcome.

The first constraint is to assume that the incumbent party is forced to fight each election on its record, and is unable to change from package to package at will. In this case, an incumbent party facing cyclical preferences in the electorate would be bound to lose every election. Whatever position the incumbent was committed to, the challenger could always find an alternative which commanded majority support. Thus, if the incumbent party had implemented a defence package, the challenger would promise a health package. If the incumbent had implemented a health package, the challenger would promise an environment package, and so on. To the extent that incumbents are stuck with the packages they have actually put into practice, this argument throws light on one of the inherent disadvantages of fighting elections as the incumbent. Downs himself discusses this when referring to the ability of the challenger, in certain circumstances, to build a 'coalition of minorities', in order to defeat an incumbent who is necessarily committed to a particular programme.[2] Downs probably rather overstresses the degree of consensus in the electorate necessary to avoid this built-in disadvantage of incumbency,[3] but the potential for cyclical majorities does demonstrate the way in which politicians can damage themselves by nailing their colours to the mast (and governments must always do this to a certain extent).

Indeterminacy is also avoided in those circumstances where the preferences of the electorate do not produce cyclical majorities. In this case, if there are two packages on offer, there will be a single package which commands majority support. This will make a government which has settled upon this package much more difficult to defeat, since the best a challenger can do is to adopt a very similar package, and fight the election either on details or on the issue of competence. There is, therefore, a sense in which competition between two rivals will either be indeterminate or degenerate. If there are cyclical majorities, there are two possibilities. The outcome may be the indeterminate conclusion of a continuous round of musical policies, determined largely by when, precisely, the music stopped. Alternatively, this indeterminacy may be constrained if one of the participants, and this will probably be the incumbent, is forced to make some sort of commitment. In this case, the rather degenerate outcome is the almost inevitable defeat of whoever has made the commitment. If there are no cyclical majorities, both contestants will adopt almost identical policy packages and fight the election on details, an outcome which also looks rather degenerate.

The degeneration of two-party competition into convergence by both contestants on a single policy package is perhaps Downs's best known deduction; but it produces a problem which is even more serious than that of indeterminacy. If small costs are involved in voting, and the voter's decision to turn out is relatively marginal, as we have argued, then two-party convergence removes the major incentive to go out and vote, which is to have some influence on the result. If voting is conducted in order to influence the outcome of the election, and if the alternatives on offer are identical, then nothing can make any difference. In these circumstances, voting will not be cost-effective, and rational individuals will not vote.

Downs extricates himself from these problems with his assumption of a single dimension of party and voter ideology. He deduces a justification for this in terms of the parties' desire to reduce the information and decision costs of the electorate. It is clear, however, that a single dimension of ideology, along which policy packages can be arrayed, both eliminates the possibility of cyclical sets of preferences in the electorate, and provides a framework for considering the circumstances in which two parties will not converge on the same policies. In these circumstances, voting will still be rational.

It is simply impossible to construct cyclical sets of preferences which can be represented on a single dimension of ideology. Any set of preferences which is effectively cyclical, having a cyclical subset which dominates all other elements, will also require more than one dimension for its representation. The most important effect of considering only a single dimension of voter and party ideology is, therefore, to impose a significant new constraint on the structure of the preferences of the electorate, by eliminating those cyclical sets which yield indeterminate results. This is not, of course, the purpose of the assumption as Downs introduces it. Furthermore, the assumption of a single dimension of ideology does not follow directly from restricting voters' preferences to those concerned with the maximization of economic well-being. The example we used above, with voters respectively preferring defence, health and environmental expenditure, is predicated on the assumption that, for various reasons, these groups perceive these policies to be the best way of realizing their economic goals. Despite this, it is quite possible to construct cyclical sets of preferences from these three elements. Is the assumption of a single dimension of voter ideology reasonable?

One potential justification of the assumption that the preferences of voters with respect to public goods packages can be represented as a single dimension arises from consideration of possible bases for raising tax revenue. If the system of taxation is progressive, then a single dimension may be a fair representation of preferences. A progressive system of taxation would assess the contribution of each individual on the basis of some criterion, such as wealth or income, with a higher level of contributions being due from those with a higher score on that criterion. A progressive system of taxation will always be approved by a majority of the population if the distribution of the population with respect to that criterion is skewed so that the majority of the population has less than the average income, wealth or whatever. This is because the production of public goods on the basis of a progressive system of taxation is redistributive, since the same value is made available to everyone from a given level of production of public goods, by definition, yet different people are paying different levels of contribution. In these circumstances, it will always be possible to set a level of public goods provision and contributions which yields a net benefit for the majority of the population with low income or wealth, on the basis of higher contributions from, and quite possibly a net loss to, the minority of the population with above-average income or wealth.

However, a majority of the population should support a system of progressive taxation and, furthermore, support increases in the level of public expenditure until a point is reached at which the net benefits accruing to them are almost exceeded by costs. When this point is reached, all those with higher levels of income or wealth will be deriving a net loss from public expenditure, since they receive the same levels of utility from the goods themselves, and pay more for them. In general terms, the evaluation by individual voters of a particular public goods package will depend directly on where they stand in the progressive tax structure. The higher the level of public goods provision, financed on the basis of progressive taxation, the more it will be valued by those at the bottom of the scale, because of the redistributive effects involved, and the more it will consequently be detested by those at the top end of the tax system. (These people will also favour private provision, where possible, because no redistribution is involved.) In short, if a unidimensional criterion is used to assess tax payments, evaluation of any given level of public goods provision may also be represented along a single dimension. As long as this criterion does not directly correspond with the level of coercive resources possessed by each voter, such a tax system will be approved by a majority vote. The dimension will represent the level of public expenditure preferred by each voter, given his consequent tax liability.

Of course, a single dimension representing tax liability for any given public goods package will closely correspond to the left–right, socio-economic dimension used by Downs. We will be able to use this dimension to represent the preferences of the electorate with respect to most public goods financed on the basis of progressively raised tax revenue. Other goods not produced on this basis, such as linguistic, ethnic or religious goods, cannot be represented on this dimension, and may generate cyclical majorities. For the moment, however, we will follow Downs, and consider competition between parties conducted on the basis of the manipulation of policies along a single dimension of ideology. Firstly, we return to the problem of the degenerate competition between two parties when each attempts to put forward the same, vote-maximizing policy. There are a number of factors which might constrain this tendency. These relate to our assumptions about voting behaviour and the formation of parties.

We have already seen that, as far as the logic of voting is concerned, the act of turning up at the polling-booth becomes less likely to be cost-effective the higher the costs of voting, and the lower the difference between the pay-offs offered by the respective contenders. Thus, as two parties converge on the same policies, the attractiveness of voting will decline. Fewer people will vote, because the benefits derived from casting an effective vote become less. This decline in turn-out will affect both parties equally, unless they are differently placed to respond to it. We can make some deductions which suggest that the parties will in fact be differently placed.

The first concerns the marginal opportunity costs of voting. If different voters have different stocks of resources and different preferences, then the resources consumed by the process of voting will involve different opportunity costs. Other things being equal, we might plausibly deduce that voters with smaller stocks of resources are likely to perceive higher opportunity costs to be associated with this particular expenditure than those with larger stocks of resources. This involves some assumption of a diminishing marginal utility arising from expenditure in general. Those with smaller stocks of resources are more likely to perceive certain objects of expenditure as essential goods. Those voters who have insufficient or barely sufficient stocks of resources to realize what they consider to be essential goals are less likely to involve themselves in voting costs than those who possess a surplus of resources over and above the level pre-empted by essential, inelastic expenditure.

The basic resources consumed by voting will be time, money and intellectual effort. Thus, people for whom these resources are at a premium relative to their perceived needs will be less likely to vote than others. It is quite possible that these people will not be equally likely to cast their votes for either of two competing parties. If we consider money, for example, then getting to the polling-point may involve some financial cost. Poor people may be more likely to support one particular public goods package than another (we have just seen that an income or wealth-based system of taxation is likely to ensure this). In these circumstances, the party offering the package which is more attractive to poor people will be at a relative disadvantage if the packages on offer converge on each other, and the benefits of voting decrease. The convergence of party policies will make the poorer people less likely to support the package they favour, since they will be less inclined to bear the costs of voting. The same will be true for parties whose packages appeal to those for whom the other resources consumed by voting are at a premium. In short, the calculus of voting may well not be the same for every voter in the system. For the reasons outlined above, different voters, preferring different types of public goods package, may be differently inclined to turn out and vote, given a particular choice of policies. This may in turn mean that the different parties suffer differently if their policies converge too closely, and it may provide some parties with an incentive to avoid such convergence.

This process is unlikely to prevent convergence in two-party competition, since the losses of one party will be effective gains for its opponent. Just as one party may have an interest in avoiding convergence of policies, the other will have a consequent interest in capitalizing on it and exaggerating the trend. Different propensities on the part of different sections of the electorate to turn out and vote for different packages will affect party competition and the likely outcome of the election. This is, however, unlikely to reverse the tendency for the politics of the only two parties in the system to become increasingly similar.

We have already seen that parties have an incentive to help voters with the costs of turning out. They can expend resources on packaging information, transporting voters to the polling-point and so on. The ability of parties to do this will, of course, depend on the resources at their disposal to cover campaign costs. These resources may well be differentially available to different parties. Parties with more campaign resources will thus be able to go further towards meeting the voting costs of their supporters. When policies converge, richer parties will be better placed than poorer parties, since they can go further towards making up the decline in expectations suffered by their supporters. This will not reverse the tendency for convergence, but will mean that convergence of policies will tend to help rich parties.

Another way of looking at this is to argue that, as policies converge and the benefits of voting decrease, then voters cut more corners in making their decision in order to reduce costs. They will move away from maximizing-decisions towards satisficing ones. If we assume that voters in this position are more susceptible to campaigning by parties – which provides them with all sorts of free information to feed into their decision calculus – then those parties with the resources to campaign vigorously will have an incentive to reduce the gap between the policies on offer. The smaller this gap, the more effective their campaigning.

One aspect of the financing of campaign expenditure may prevent convergence of policies, however. Parties, as we have seen, will expend resources on informing their potential supporters of their programme. If we assume that this expenditure increases when the party changes its policies, then *any* change in policy, including a convergence on an opponent's policies, may not be worth the consequent benefits. We have seen that campaign funds are likely to be forthcoming only if the recipient has some chance of becoming the incumbent. But campaign funds can be used for many purposes. If the extra campaign costs involved in changing policies yield fewer additional votes than other forms of campaign expenditure, then changing party policy may be less productive than spending the funds elsewhere. If changing party policy involves no cost, the behaviour of the electorate is unlikely to constrain the convergence of party policy. But since policy changes are costly, they may not be worth it.

As well as adding to campaign costs, any change in a party's policy may undermine its credibility with the electorate. We have seen that voters will make their decision on the basis of their evaluation of the value and credibility of the policy packages on offer. If we assume that they are likely to regard a party's policies as less credible if they are frequently changed, then any particular policy change will lose votes as well as gain them. This in itself may prevent a party from moving its policies towards those of its opponent. In general, therefore, policy changes may cost campaign funds and votes, and maximization may therefore dictate the retention of distinct policy positions, even in two-party systems.

Finally, we earlier made the assumption that the *perceived* difference between the same two policies may be less, the further these policies are from a given voter's own preferred position. If this assumption is correct, then voters at the extremes of the policy spectrum may well stop voting for the party of their choice, despite the fact that it still offers them policies which are closer to the ones they prefer than the policies offered by opponents. As policies converge on the centre, a point may be reached at which any further move loses more votes than it gains, as a disproportionate number of voters at the extremes decide that the difference between the packages on offer does not merit the costs of voting. This may inhibit either party from taking the initiative in moving its policies towards the centre, once this point has been reached, since the move would incur directly consequential losses of voters.

A more plausible set of constraints on the impulses of parties to converge on the centre ground can be derived, however, from a consideration of intra-party politics. These arguments were not, of course, available to Downs, given his assumption that parties function as unitary actors.

Subsequent authors, including Hirschman and Robertson, have produced a number of arguments concerning the effects of parties' internal organization.[4] Both discuss the consequences of the ways in which resources are made available to parties, Hirschman concentrating on party workers, and Robertson on financial sponsorship. Both show that, if a party's ability to attract these resources affects its ability to win votes, and if its policies affect its ability to attract resources, then its vote-maximizing position is not necessarily the one which is most popular with the electorate. Each party will then need to trade off its appeal to the electorate against its ability (in terms of resources) to transform this appeal into actual votes.

Our discussion of the ways in which public entrepreneurs and political parties can raise funds to meet campaign costs provides some deductive justification for these arguments in terms of rational choice theory. (They are presented by Hirschman and Robertson more as plausible generalizations from the real world.) We saw that politicians can attract support from aspiring suppliers of the factors of production of public goods. We also saw that these suppliers will have an interest in underwriting the organization costs of pressure groups, if the activity of these groups is likely to modify the public goods package eventually enacted. This is because different public goods packages are likely to provide different benefits for different suppliers. These suppliers will therefore have an interest, when providing some of parties' campaign costs, in the precise policies they will enact if elected. They will want parties to enact the public goods package which yields them the greatest profit. There is no reason to assume that the most profitable package as far as the suppliers are concerned will in any way correspond to the policy preferred by the median voter. If parties can deploy campaign funds to transform potential support into actual support, then they may be able to adopt relatively unpopular policies and still win the election, if these policies generate sufficient campaign funds to offset the vote losses arising from failure to adopt the most popular policy. This will tend to pull parties away from the policy preferred by the median voter, and towards the policy preferred by their financial sponsors.[5] The cheaper the campaign contributions, relative to the private benefits for the contributor if the recipient succeeds, and the more marginal the voters' decisions, the more significantly the structure of campaign funding will affect the relationships between potential support and actual support. The more important campaign funding is, the more likely it is that parties will adopt policies which maximize votes received, but are not the most popular with the electorate.

Potential suppliers of the factors of production of public goods are not, however, the only people who may make significant gains as a result of changes in public policy. Different individuals will be differently affected by different packages of public goods. If campaign contributions can affect the level of votes actually received by a party, it is possible that private individuals who are severely disadvantaged by one (relatively popular) package rather than another (relatively unpopular) one, may attempt to influence party policy, making conditional campaign contributions which offset the loss of votes produced by adopting the less popular policy. Thus, a major producer in the private goods market may run a very profitable enterprise which pollutes the environment. An entrepreneur or party may see a potential surplus in the advocacy of anti-pollution legislation, producing a public good by banning the pollution. This public good would be a private bad for the polluter, but the policy might potentially be very popular. If the polluter made campaign contributions to the party which were conditional upon it dropping its anti-pollution policy, the party may be adequately compensated and comply. Anyone whose private interests in the effects of public policy are sufficiently large may find it rational to make campaign contributions, in the expectation of modifying party policy.

All of this shows that the sources of campaign finance may encourage parties to adopt policies which maximize votes without being popular. This will happen when campaign costs are relatively low, because voters' decisions are relatively marginal when they compare the costs of voting with the likely benefits. These low campaign costs can be met by suppliers or other private individuals, for whom the consequences of different public goods packages are relatively important.

Hirschman makes broadly the same argument about the effect of party activists on party policy.[6] The resource contributed by activists is labour, and such a contribution may be rational to the extent that it can produce a consequential shift in party policy. If activists withhold their support when the party adopts policies that they do not like, and give it when they approve, then the party may once more maximize votes by adopting unpopular policies, to the extent that it is compensated by the extra labour it receives, which helps to turn potential votes into actual votes.

To conclude this discussion, we have seen that in a two-party system there will be a tendency for the contenders to converge on the centre of the ideological spectrum, which is the position producing the greatest potential support. Consequent decline in turn-out is likely to mean that this process will help some parties and harm others. But constraints on convergence emerge from a consideration of the costs, both of informing the electorate and in maintaining credibility, which may simply not be worth the consequent benefits. Furthermore, campaign funds may themselves be supplied to the parties on condition that the policies adopted are not those with the greatest potential support.

MORE PARTIES

Many important features of party competition can be discussed with reference to a system consisting of only two contenders. Comparing two-party and multi-party systems, the most obvious difference is that competition between two parties for the support of a majority of the electorate is effectively zero sum. Either one party or the other will win, and one party's gains will be entirely at the expense of the other. When there are more than two parties, this is not the case. Any two parties may each gain at the expense of a third and will therefore have common, as well as conflicting, interests. Associated with this is the possibility that, when more than two parties contest the election, no single party will achieve a majority of the votes cast. It may therefore be necessary, after the election, for the parties to form coalitions in order to command majority support. Coalitions will be discussed further in the following chapter, but it is worth noting at this point that the ability of a party to include itself in the winning coalition will depend partly on its voting strength, but also on the policies it is advocating. A party will be a more welcome addition to a proto-coalition if its policies are close to coalition policy. Parties will therefore be forced to consider the effects of their policies on their coalition bargaining position as well as on their electoral popularity. Vote-maximizing positions may not maximize a party's chances of getting into power. A particular change in policy could lose votes, but put the party in a superior bargaining position.

Consider firstly the potential for electoral cooperation in a competitive multi-party system. We can show that, paradoxically, such cooperation can counteract tendencies for party policies to converge upon one another. If two parties are adjacent to one another on the policy scale, and if each faces competition on its other ideological flank, then it may well be rational for these parties to agree *not* to converge on one another. The parties will gain more votes if they keep their distance from one another, rather than converge, thereby losing votes to the rivals on their other flanks. There are no circumstances in which they increase their combined support by agreeing to converge ideologically, since this simply narrows the basis of their appeal, throwing away votes to mutual rivals. In policy terms, therefore, electoral agreements between parties are likely to involve the parties keeping their distance ideologically, and agreeing not to exploit the ideological gap between them. Electoral agreements are unlikely to result in the convergence of party policy. Thus, to the extent that the parties in a multi-party system make explicit or tacit agreements with one another, the tendencies for ideological convergence may be reduced. This will particularly affect ideological convergence in the centre of the spectrum, since the parties of the extreme will have nothing to gain from making such deals. Extreme parties should not make agreements with their ideological neighbours, since they lose no votes by entering into ruthless ideological competition with them. While ideological collusion between parties may stop convergence on the centre ground, it should leave competition at the extremes of the policy spectrum as intense as ever.

In contrast to this, consideration of their post-electoral bargaining strength may make parties want to converge ideologically.

Coalitions will tend to form between parties with relatively similar policies, because the costs involved are less than for coalitions between parties which span a wide ideological range. Parties will be liable to lose votes if they do not put into practice the packages that they have promised their supporters, since these supporters will evaluate the credibility of the packages at least partly on the basis of past performance. Parties will therefore be unwilling to promise packages which they will be forced to abandon in order to get into power by entering coalition. It will thus make sense for parties to anticipate the coalitions which are likely to form, and to take account of these when constructing their policy packages. In certain circumstances, therefore, parties may put forward packages which are closer to those of some of their rivals than would otherwise be the case, because these rivals are also potential coalition partners. This process will not be confined to the centre of the policy spectrum, since all parties will want to get into power and will be prepared to make the necessary compromises. The effects of parties anticipating likely post-electoral coalitions will, however, be more predictable at the extremes of the policy spectrum than it will be at the centre. Parties at the extremes can only make their compromises in one direction, towards the centre. This will reinforce the tendency produced by the unattractiveness of electoral coalitions to extreme parties. Each tendency encourages these parties to converge on their closest ideological rivals. In the centre of the policy spectrum, the situation will be much less clear-cut, although centre parties may well tend to converge on their stronger rivals, since these will be more likely than others to be members of winning coalitions.

If changes of policy involve costs in terms of both credibility and campaign funds, then this will tend to exert a dampening effect on the whole process of ideological manoeuvring by parties. In particular, parties may not respond to shifts of preference in the electorate, or to likely coalitions which they expect to be short-lived. If the short-term benefits, in terms of the expectations of office, are outweighed by the long-term costs, in terms of credibility and campaign funds sacrificed if party policy will have to be changed again in the opposite direction, then a particular policy change which might appear attractive if a party was fighting the last election in the world will be less so when it considers its long-term future. This may well constrain centre parties' tendencies to converge on potential coalition partners; they may not change their public goods package if they expect that this will make them even less attractive to other, future, coalition partners.

In conclusion, the existence of three or more competing parties will create a potential for cooperation, as well as conflict, even in a highly competitive system. Pre-electoral coalitions may be mutually beneficial to their members, although they will not include parties at the extremes of the ideological scale. Pre-electoral coalitions will tend to counteract the tendency for convergence on a single, vote-maximizing policy. All parties may want to modify their electoral packages in anticipation of potential post-electoral coalitions. Parties at the extremes will have an incentive to do this, and their policies consequently will tend to move towards the centre of the policy scale. If changing policies involves costs, this will tend to dampen the whole process.

Thus the equivalent of two-party convergence on a single, vote-maximizing policy is a tendency for the range of policies advocated in a multi-party system to contract at either extreme of the scale, since these parties always have an incentive to move in on their closest rivals. Centre parties may, however, offer a range of different policies. These conclusions correspond to Downs's discussion of stable ideological configurations in multi-party systems. His deduction that three-party systems will tend to be unstable, for example, is consistent with our argument that constraints on convergence will not apply to the parties at the extremes of the ideological spectrum, since two of the three parties will inevitably be at these extremes and converge on the centre. In these circumstances, the only constraints on convergence will be those which exist for a two-party system, arising from the demand for and supply of campaign funds. For systems with four or more parties, there will be two or more parties in the centre. These will have both the incentive and the means to ensure that ideological convergence does not damage them too seriously. In these circumstances, competition at the extremes is likely to be more intense than competition at the centre, but stable ideological configurations may well emerge. Large parties in the centre will tend to exert a sort of gravitational pull on their smaller neighbours, as these view them as potentially crucial to any coalition of which they are members and modify their policies accordingly.

NEW PARTIES

We have so far been assuming implicitly that it is not possible for new parties to enter the fray. This is clearly unwarranted, given the potentially large rewards of winning elections, or at least of belonging to winning coalitions. The possibility that new parties will enter the market will clearly influence those parties which are already there. New parties will, in general, enter the market only if they have some expectation of either winning the election or belonging to a winning coalition. This means that the decision to enter the market will depend on three things: the costs of entry, the level of potential support – and hence the probability of success – and the benefits of success. (An important exception to this will be discussed below.)

The costs of entry into the market will depend on a number of things, and will appear mainly in the form of campaign expenditure. Obviously, the higher the level of campaign expenditure required for a given probability of success, the less attractive is entering the campaign. This will in part depend on the level of campaign expenditure of the other parties; the more other parties are spending, the more, other things being equal, a new party will have to spend. In a highly competitive system, the existing parties may have very high campaign budgets compared to the budgets in a relatively uncompetitive system, where the parties are effectively colluding. This will make intervention in a competitive system more expensive, and hence less attractive, than intervention in an uncompetitive system. Conversely, the threat of new parties will constrain the desire of existing parties to collude.

The impact of campaign costs on entry could mean that existing parties will keep costs high to act as a deterrent to new entrants, or even force poorer existing competitors out of business. It is clear that the higher the campaign costs, the lower the ideological diversity of the policies on offer, since all barriers to entry reduce the threat of new ideological competitors to the established parties.

There will be other, non-recurrent, entry costs which will concern the need of a new party to make its presence and its policy package known to potential supporters. These costs will not bother existing parties whose presence and policies will already be familiar. The higher these costs are, the less attractive is the contest to a new party. Non-recurrent 'break-in' costs will vary very much from system to system. The higher these costs are, however, the greater the attractiveness of collusion between the existing parties, because the lower the chance of new rivals.

The probability of a successful intervention will depend in part on the nature of any 'gaps in the market', groups of voters to which no party is offering any attractive public goods package, and in part on the precise voting system used. Both the size and the position of gaps in the market will be important. The size of any gaps will obviously depend on the number of parties in the system and the policy packages that they are offering. Other things being equal, the size of the largest pool of voters who would prefer an alternative policy package to any which is already on offer will determine the likelihood of a successful new entry. The more policy packages on offer, the smaller this pool will be, and the lower the probability of success for a new entrant. For a given entry cost, therefore, the likelihood of a new party entering the fray will increase as the number of existing parties decreases. The more parties there already are, the less likely is a new entry.

The particular policies advocated by the existing parties will also have an important effect on this process. For a given distribution of electoral preference, the more diverse the policy packages offered by existing parties, the smaller the pools of voters preferring alternatives. The more the policy packages have tended to converge, the larger the pools of voters who may prefer alternative policies. The simple example in Figure 3 describes alternative ideological configurations for a four-party system with an even distribution of voters across the scale. In Situation I, the parties A, B,

C and D adopt diverse policy packages. Each will receive 25 per cent of the vote, if voters support the party whose policy package is closest to their own preferred outcome. The most profitable points for a new party to intervene in the competition are at X and Y. A party which could convince the electorate that it would enact these policies would receive 15 per cent of the votes. This configuration provides less scope for intervention than Situation II, which might emerge after the two parties on the extremes, A and D, had converged on the centre, and the centre parties, B and C, had responded. The voting strength of the parties would be unchanged after all of this, at 25 per cent of the total for each party, but the gaps in the market would be wider. There will be three points, X', Y' and Z', at which an intervening party could offer a policy which would be supported by almost 25 per cent of the voters. For a given intervention cost, entry would be far more attractive.

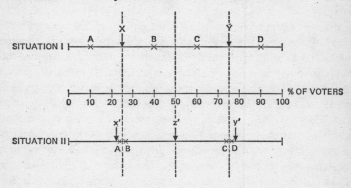

FIG. 3: EASE OF ENTRY INTO A FOUR-PARTY SYSTEM
Assuming a single dimension of ideology.

This example highlights another important aspect of the possibility of new parties intervening in the system. The threat of intervention will obviously act as a constraint on the ideological competition of the existing parties. If the probability of intervention is materially affected by the move from Situation I to Situation II, then parties may be more reluctant to make the move. More significantly, we see that the parties instigating the move, the extreme parties A and D, are most seriously affected by any intervention. Intervention at the extremes will come from parties adopting policies which are very similar to their own, effectively robbing them of almost all of their support. This will always be the case for the extreme parties, since they will be the source of all votes lost as a result of interventions, whereas centre parties will share the damage. Thus, the threat of intervention will act as an important constraint on the tendency of extreme parties to converge on the centre of the system, and will in general encourage a wider diversity in the policy packages on offer than would otherwise be the case. Since the threat of intervention will also be a function of entry costs, the lower the entry costs, other things being equal, the more the extreme parties will be constrained, and the more diverse will be the policy packages on offer. Conversely, systems with high entry costs will tend to have less ideological diversity, with extreme parties converging on the centre.

Different systems of counting votes will affect the way in which potential support is transformed into electoral strength. Systems which are very proportional will convert potential support into electoral strength more effectively, particularly for small parties, than systems which are not. Since, for a given entry cost and ideological configuration, anticipated electoral success will affect the probability of intervention, proportional electoral systems will yield higher probabilities of electoral success, and therefore increase the probability of intervention. Since the probability of intervention, as we have just seen, affects the nature of ideological competition between the existing parties, proportional electoral systems will tend to have the same effect as low entry costs. Thus, the more proportional the electoral system, the greater the incentive for extreme parties to stay at the extremes, and the greater the diversity of the policy packages on offer. Less proportional systems will tend to have the opposite effect, encouraging extreme parties to converge on the centre, and generally restricting ideological diversity.

The final factor affecting the probability of intervention in party competition is the level of surplus which will be retained by a potential competitor if intervention is successful. This will depend on two things; the overall level of surplus arising from public goods provision, and the number of parties between which this surplus must be shared. The overall level of available surplus will decrease with increasing competitiveness in the system, and increase with increasing collusion between participants. The higher the level of competition, and the less collusion there is, the lower the level of retained surplus, and hence the lower the probability of intervention. When majority support can only be commanded by a coalition of parties, members of the winning coalition will have to share the retained surplus. The possibility of joining a coalition, and of obtaining bargaining strength within that coalition, will also affect the probability that a potential new party will decide that intervention costs represent a worthwhile investment. This will be another reason why intervention becomes less attractive, the more parties there are in the system, since the rewards of office will have to be spread more thinly. It will further make intervention in the centre of the policy spectrum rather more attractive than intervention at the extremes, since centre parties will have more potential coalition partners, and hence a higher probability of belonging to a winning coalition (see Chapter 6). Thus, while voting strength may be increased by intervention at the extremes, as we saw above, a given voting strength may yield higher expectations at the centre, making interventions at the centre more likely.

In conclusion, the probability that new parties will enter the system in competition for the incumbency will depend on entry costs, the number of parties in the system, the precise policies that these parties are advocating, the electoral system and the rewards of office. The possibility of intervention will constrain the existing parties, producing greater ideological diversity than would otherwise be the case. Anything which increases the probability of intervention should also, other things being equal, increase ideological diversity, and reduce the tendency of extreme parties to converge on the centre of the system.

As a postscript to this discussion, we should consider a type of intervention which is not intended to capture the incumbency, and which is explained directly from our existing conclusions. Since interventions and potential interventions have the effect of modifying the policies of the existing parties, they may be threatened or enacted to achieve precisely this effect, even if those involved have no chance of capturing the incumbency. Suppliers of factors of production of public goods, and other individuals or organizations who would derive significant private benefits as a result of a change in public policy, may field candidates whose purpose is solely to modify policy by forcing the existing parties to take account of the electoral threat posed by their new challenger. The lower the entry costs into the system, the more likely is this possibility, which modifies the ideological outcome of party competition. Since the threat of entry may be just as effective as the entry itself, public policy may be modified in this way without actually contesting elections. Those politicians who enter the system in order to modify the eventual policies enacted will not necessarily be vote-maximizers. Their very existence in the system should guarantee some modification in policy; they may thus be sponsored by individuals or organizations of individuals who have a private interest in achieving this. Because these politicians are not vote-maximizers, they will not necessarily attempt to produce the most popular policies, although they must pose a threat to the popularity of the parties they wish to influence. Thus, politicians who are not vote-maximizers may realize a surplus on the basis of contributions from sponsors, and may reward those sponsors with real benefits in terms of modification of public policy, even though they never come close to achieving power.

With this important exception, however, party competition will tend to result in a relative lack of diversity in the policies offered. This is caused by the desire of politicians who are eager for the rewards of the incumbency to produce popular policies. The trend towards ideological convergence will be counteracted to some extent by factors affecting campaign financing, and the threat of entry by new parties. Ideological convergence may be further restrained by the existence of parties who are not interested in achieving power, but rather in modifying other parties' policies on behalf of their sponsors. As a very general summary of all our conclusions, we can say behaviour aimed at pleasing the electorate tends to produce a search for the most popular policy, which reduces the range of options on offer; however, behaviour aimed at pleasing sponsors tends to have the opposite effect, since it will be rational for sponsors to intervene only to the extent that their intervention produces an outcome which would not prevail if policies were selected on the basis of their popularity.

POLITICIANS' POLICY PREFERENCES

Thus far, the argument has mainly concerned politicians whose primary instrumental goal is vote-maximization. Vote-maximization increases the chance of a politician participating in the incumbency and consequently realizing a *production* surplus as a result of public goods provision. We have ignored the *consumption* preferences of politicians since, in most circumstances, this surplus will be smaller than that arising from producing public goods at a profit. We have assumed that politicians produce whatever public goods package is necessary to maximize their chance of success at elections, regardless of their personal preferences about public goods consumption. There are, however, certain circumstances in which the personal consumption preferences of politicians will influence their choice of policies. When competition for the support of a *particular* group of consumers is intense, public goods production surpluses will be pared to the bare minimum. (Competition for the loyalty of different groups of consumers will not have this effect.) With production surpluses pared to the bare minimum, the public goods consumption preferences of politicians will play a more important role in the cost-benefit calculations which determine the policies they offer. In these circumstances, the policies of parties will be partially determined by the preferences of their members.

To the extent that it remains necessary to succeed at elections in order to influence the policies which are actually put into practice, party policy must still be popular. At the margin, however, a given change in policy may not affect a party's chance of success, and may thus be adopted because it is preferred by party members. This is particularly likely to happen in two circumstances, the first of which arises when the party concerned expects to gain a clear majority at the following election. Those votes in excess of a majority of all votes cast will be surplus to requirements. Once a majority vote has been secured, vote-maximization ceases to be an instrumental goal, and alternative strategies more effectively maximize politicians' utility income. They will do better to move party policy towards their own preferences, at the expense of votes, provided that their majority is not endangered. Utility-maximization is served by vote-maximization only until a majority of votes is received; after this point, utility may be further increased by adopting those policies which are preferred by party members.

If the expected result of the election is that no party will achieve an overall majority, then a coalition of parties will be necessary before a package can be constructed which has majority support. In these circumstances, parties will be concerned with their post-electoral bargaining power, since it is this which affects their chances of participating in the incumbency. Obviously, the maximization of bargaining power and the maximization of votes will be closely related, since an increase in the total of votes received can never reduce, and will often increase, bargaining power. There will be many inceases in votes received, however, which have no effect on bargaining power, and such increases will not be instrumentally rational. For example, if three parties each received one third of the votes, any one of them may gain or lose substantial quantities of votes without affecting their consequent bargaining power. Provided that, in the end, *any two* of the parties are still essential to a majority coalition, then the bargaining power of each party will be unchanged. In these circumstances, vote-maximization will not always be the best way of maximizing utility, since votes can be lost without affecting their losers' utility expectations, provided that bargaining power is not eroded. Parties may thus modify policies at the expense of votes, and in accord with the consumption preferences of members, if this does not cost them bargaining leverage in the coalition negotiations. Thus, in multi-party systems in which coalitions are expected, party policy may be partially determined by the preferences of members.

Deviations from vote-maximizing policies in accord with the

private consumption preferences of politicians are thus likely either when a single party expects votes in excess of a majority, or when coalitions are likely and some parties can lose votes without losing bargaining power. This, of course, covers most eventualities, the main exception being closely contested two-party confrontations, when politicians will be forced to look for the most popular policies, regardless of their personal preferences concerning public goods production. Vote-maximization will remain the dominant instrumental strategy in all circumstances in which the main way of influencing public policy is by participating in the incumbency. The point of this discussion is to show that, once vote-maximization has produced the maximum possible increase in the expectation of power, the utility income of politicians may be further increased by some modification of party policy in accord with their personal preferences.

There is one further possible reason for politicians to adopt the policies which they prefer rather than the policies which are most popular. This arises when there are many suppliers of factors of production prepared to underwrite campaign costs. If these suppliers have a diverse range of interests in public policy, and if the campaign expenditure they underwrite can increase actual, as opposed to potential, support for less popular policies, then politicians may choose their sponsors in accord with their personal public goods preferences. We have seen that the suppliers of campaign funds can influence public policy, because they can influence the rate at which potential support is transformed into real support, given the calculus of voting problem. If there are more suppliers who are prepared to do this than are required by politicians, there is no reason why politicians should not behave so that any deviations from vote-maximizing policies which take place as a result of this redound to their own benefit. If there is a correspondence of interest between some politicians and some suppliers, then these will be drawn to one another, since both groups will derive benefits from the same, less popular, policies. Between them they will have the means to put these policies into practice. In short, if there are more suppliers of campaign funds than are necessary, politicians may be able to enact policies they prefer if they can choose suppliers who want the same policies and who will help them overcome any losses of potential support. These policies will, of course, be vote-maximizing policies, although they will not necessarily be popular policies.

6 Some Thoughts on Coalitions

When no single party gains a majority at an election, it will be necessary to form a coalition of parties in order to produce a viable public goods package. Coalition theory has been a major focus of activity for rational choice theorists for some time, and owes much to the early contributions of William Riker.[1] An extended discussion of this writing here would represent a major digression, however, and I shall discuss only those matters which bear directly on the arguments advanced in the preceding chapters.

We have already assumed that parties which go into government will be assessed by the electorate in terms of their performance in office and the policies which they actually put into practice. They will lose votes at subsequent elections if they make a mess of things or if they adopt unpopular policies. If this assumption also applies to members of coalition cabinets as well as to one-party incumbencies, then the precise policy package likely to be adopted by a coalition will be an important consideration in each party's decision to join. Since parties will have only limited ability to control the policy of a coalition government, it is reasonable to infer that they will be unwilling to enter a coalition which is likely to prove a subsequent electoral liability. This will hold true unless the perceived short-term rewards of a single period in office outweigh any further losses of popularity. At this stage, therefore, we are forced to make assumptions about the time horizons of potential coalition members.

A week in politics may be a long time for some. They may heavily discount any long-term benefits of particular actions, either because they are unconcerned about their future utility or because they regard the future as too unpredictable to be worth taking into consideration. Other politicians may regard long-term prospects as being of paramount importance, and do nothing in the short-term which is likely to jeopardize these. Politicians with an eye to the future will not want to join unpopular coalitions, but politicians who discount future utility income quite steeply are much less likely to be concerned with the effect of coalition policy on electoral success. Those who are not prepared to look as far as the next election may perceive no disadvantage, on policy grounds, in joining any coalition, and go along with whatever is necessary to get a seat in the cabinet chamber, however unpopular this might be with the electorate.

Politicians may also be concerned with coalition policy because of the way in which the electorate treats a party which promises one thing at an election, and goes on to join a coalition which actually does something else. If parties are punished by voters for doing this, because of their reduced electoral credibility, then they will not be inclined to enter coalitions which will enact policies that differ drastically from their own. Assuming that politicians do not totally discount their prospects at subsequent elections, they will prefer to enter coalitions which enact policies which are relatively popular, and which do not significantly deviate from their own. The concern of coalition theories with party policy does depend, therefore, upon an assumption that politicians are relatively far-sighted.

If this is the case, then parties at the centre of the policy spectrum will be more inclined to go into coalitions than parties at the extremes. This is because policies at the extremes of the spectrum are more likely to be easily bettered by more popular policies. Any move towards the centre should increase the popularity of coalition policy, for the same reasons as it increases the popularity of policies put forward by single parties. There will usually be more votes to be gained than lost by such a move. The centripetal ideological tendencies of coalition policy may, if anything, be greater than those for a single party, since at least one of the constraints on single-party convergence will not apply to coalitions. The threat posed by new entrants will be much less for coalitions. While a new entrant at the extremes of the party scale could almost destroy a single party, damage to a coalition will be worse for the member in closest ideological proximity to the intervention. While such an intervention may destroy a hitherto winning coalition, the spread of policies preferred by coalition members will cushion those effects. No single intervention against a coalition with a spread of policies can be as effective as an intervention against a party with a discrete position on the policy scale.

Policies located in the centre of the spectrum will also have the electoral advantage that those who oppose them will not be able to agree on a preferred alternative. If parties have perfect information about the preferences of the electorate, and if voting costs are ignored, then the only coalition policy which cannot be defeated is the policy preferred by the median voter on the policy scale. Any other coalition policy can be defeated at the very least by adopting the policy preferred by the median voter. The fact that information about preferences is not perfect, and that voting costs resources, will create uncertainty and distortions in this process as we have seen in our discussion of party competition, since there will be a number of reasons why parties need not adopt vote-maximizing policies. Other things being equal, however, there will be a tendency for more central policies to provide coalitions with greater electoral success than extreme policies. In effect, the need to adopt a single coalition policy produces a situation which is analogous to two-party competition, when the subsequent election is considered. Members of the coalition will be concerned with the relationship between coalition policy and the best alternative policy. The tendencies for convergence in two-party systems will thus also affect the formation of coalition policy. Given this tendency for coalition policy to be at the centre of the policy scale, and given the costs to parties of entering coalitions which adopt policies different from their own, then extreme parties will tend to face higher costs on entering coalitions than the parties in the centre, who will favour the sorts of policies which coalitions are likely to adopt. For a given benefit, entering coalitions is likely to be more cost-effective for centre parties. We have seen that at least one of the constraints on ideological convergence will not apply to coalitions. Potential new entrants pose less of a threat to coalitions. A number of the factors which tend to pull policy away from the centre of the scale still apply, however. These include the preferences of the suppliers of campaign funds, and the preferences, at the margin, of the politicians themselves. To the extent that parties can be compensated for adopting less popular policies, they will do so, and the centripetal tendency of coalition policy will be counteracted.

The costs to parties of adopting coalition policies different from those with which they fought the election will also tend to reduce the ideological 'spread' of coalition membership, since, for a given benefit, coalitions which are ideologically compact are likely to cost members less than coalitions which have an ideologically diverse membership.[2] The costs, of course, are mainly in terms of lost votes at the subsequent election, although the personal preferences of politicians may influence this to the extent that party policy corresponds with members' preferences, for the reasons discussed in the previous chapter. Other things being equal, politicians will go into coalitions with policies they prefer, but they will not do this in preference to going into coalitions with better long-term prospects of incumbency.

Our conclusions about the ideological aspects of coalition bargaining (that coalitions will tend to adopt central policies and will tend to be ideologically compact) thus depend upon an assumption that politicians enter coalitions with an eye to what is likely to happen at the following election. If politicians are unconcerned about the next election, because they discount future utility rather steeply, then the policies adopted by coalitions will be almost irrelevant to them. In these circumstances, they will be concerned with coalition policy only to the extent that, given two alternative winning coalitions of which they are members, they will choose the coalition which is likely to adopt a policy which corresponds to their own preferences.

Ideological aspects of coalition bargaining have been discussed in the extensive literature on coalition formation, for example by Axelrod and De Swaan, although most of these discussions regard ideology as being less important than the other principal criterion, size. The importance accorded to size can now be seen to depend upon a judgement that politicians discount future utility sufficiently steeply that they do not consider disadvantages at the following elections when deciding on whether to enter a particular coalition. In these circumstances, ideology will influence only the choice between alternative winning coalitions of which the same party is a member. The question of not entering a coalition on ideological grounds will not arise. This explains why coalition policy is usually appended as a lexicographically inferior criterion after the other factors which influence formation have been taken into account.[3] If politicians have long time-horizons, however, coalition policy may well be the most important factor that they take into consideration.

There is, however, almost universal agreement among the many authors of rational choice theories of coalition formation that size is the most important criterion which will determine membership.[4] This argument stems from Riker's writing on the subject, and is usually based on the assumption that all coalitions are of equal value. If all winning coalitions are of equal value, then small winning coalitions will be preferred to large winning coalitions, because each individual member of the small coalition stands to receive a larger proportion of the value. A somewhat weaker statement of this argument, also proposed by Riker, suggests that, even when all winning coalitions are not of equal value, winning coalitions will exclude members who are not essential to the majority. This is the so-called 'minimal winning' criterion. Redundant members contribute nothing to the strength of the coalition, can therefore expect no share of the pay-out, and hence will have no incentive to join.

This argument depends implicitly upon an assumption that politicians do not consider what is likely to happen at the next election, since, under certain circumstances, the inclusion of members whose presence in the coalition is not essential to its majority may be beneficial to the others. If coalition members are concerned with the possibility of being defeated at the next election, and if the likely level of electoral support for each coalition member depends on the actual policy enacted by the coalition, as well as on the relationship between this policy and the policy advocated at the previous election, then coalition members may reduce the threat of future opposition by incorporating potential opponents into the winning coalition. This will be particularly true for parties which advocate popular policies, but are nevertheless not essential to a particular majority. Such parties may be well placed to oppose co-alition policy at the next election, either on their own, or as part of an opposing coalition, but the danger of such opposition may clearly be reduced if the relevant party joins the incumbent ma-jority. This is effectively a form of collusion between parties, in which potential opponents are bought off with some of the rewards of incumbency. It will be particularly attractive for the winning coalition if the party in question has policies which are similar to coalition policy, since policy concessions will not be necessary. Co-alition policy may have to be changed to attract a party with quite different policies, in order to reduce its losses at the subsequent election. This argument corresponds to a position argued by Axel-rod, who suggests that winning coalitions may include surplus members, if those members have policies which are within the range of policies encompassed by essential coalition members.[5] These are so-called 'minimum connected winning' coalitions, which consist of members essential to a majority, plus those members who are not essential, but whose policies are within the range of policies advocated by essential members. This argument advanced here goes rather further, suggesting that other potentially dangerous op-ponents may be co-opted into the winning coalition, if this reduces the threat of defeat at future elections.

In conclusion, it can be seen that two important criteria which will determine the composition of the winning coalition will be the size of the coalition and the policies of its members. Traditionally, size has been considered to dominate ideology, but it can be seen that this conclusion depends upon the assumption that politicians do not give much thought to what is likely to happen at the fol-lowing election. If politicians have longer time-horizons than this, ideology may dominate size, and the policy of coalitions may become more important than the number of members. Indeed, even surplus members may be included, if this defuses future opposition. In these circumstances, not only will coalitions tend to be ideo-logically compact (the conventional conclusion), but they will also tend to adopt policies which are close to the centre of the policy scale. This is because the formation of a coalition's policies marks the start of the following election campaign, and the competition between the incumbent coalition and the strongest challenge which can be mounted resembles two-party competition, with all of the consequent tendencies for convergence. The strongest challenge to which the incumbent coalition must respond will always come from the ideological direction of the median voter. Thus, while multi-party systems will produce a wider variety of policies on offer to the electorate than two-party systems, for reasons discussed in the previous chapter, the tendency for ideological convergence on the centre ground is simply pushed one stage further along the line, and emerges in the process of deciding upon the policy of the winning coalition. In either case, in terms of actual policies enacted, the median voter on the policy scale is the person most likely to receive long-term satisfaction.

7 Conclusion

The argument in this book concerns the political implications of people's private desires for public goods. When public goods are not provided by philanthropists or philosopher-kings, they will have to come from somewhere. Indeed, we saw early on that at least one public good, some means for facilitating the making of binding agreements, is essential for the consummation of many of even the most private transactions. Furthermore, many private transactions generate public bads, and the avoidance of those will always be a matter of common concern. A concentration on the problems of providing public goods does not, therefore, necessarily presuppose an overriding concern with the *desirability* of collective consumption. It simply recognizes the inevitable collective implications of the private consumption of all types of good. The question of *which* public goods should be produced has been studiously avoided.

The metaphor used throughout has been the market. I must point out very firmly at this stage, however, that whenever I have, explicitly or implicitly, considered market mechanisms of one form or another, I have conceived of them in their very broadest sense. Markets have been discussed as means of reconciling the supply and demand for goods, and the precise medium of exchange employed has been deliberately left open. The markets of the classical economist usually depend upon the existence of some commonly valued numeraire good, such as money. The markets we have discussed involve the use of a wide range of types of exchange, which we have referred to very generally as resources. These resources might include money, but they also include time, energy, effort and skill, as well as promises and threats involving these. Thus, the markets we consider may allocate scarce goods according to how much people can pay for them, but they may also do so on the basis of how long they are prepared to wait or queue for them, or whatever else they are prepared to do or put at risk for them.

The central theme of the book has been the nature of the market in public goods, which are not susceptible to market allocation in the traditional economic sense, because they cannot easily be distributed according to the ways in which people can contribute resources towards their costs. The solutions to this problem of traditional market failure are political, depending either upon relatively informal collective organization on a conditional basis, as in the case of anarchy, or upon some form of coercion, the factor which usually distinguishes public from private entrepreneurs. I have almost certainly exaggerated this case, portraying the sole purpose of political activity as a response to the need to provide public goods. While I would not go to the stake for this position, I do feel that it is a useful exercise to see where this gets us.

Where does it get us? We started with a very general set of core assumptions about political man, which portray him as desiring a set of goals which are in short supply and behaving in such a way as to most efficiently realize these goals. We also assumed that some of these goods intrinsically involve collective consumption, while others require or invite joint production. These goods present a problem of collective action, since rational individuals will further their ends by taking 'free rides', consuming without contributing. I have deliberately ignored one possible solution to this problem, which is to devote our energy to devising means by which free-riders can be excluded. If we wish to push things to the limit, of course, it is probably true that our ingenuity would be sufficient to solve many collective action problems this way. We can set up private fire brigades and police forces, franchise our public open spaces to private entrepreneurs, replace our lighthouses with radio beacons transmitting scrambled signals and so on. We can take even the purest examples of a public good, such as the prevention of epidemics of new diseases, and puzzle over this until we find some way of confining the benefits to a predetermined group. I have ignored this possibility because I have the feeling that it is ultimately futile, if not preposterous. Public goods in some shape or form will always be with us, and the problem of providing them cannot be solved by stamping them out. Quite simply the very process of stamping them out generates public bads, and the avoidance of each of these bads is itself a public good. Anyway, some public goods, such as peace and collective defence, will always be instrumentally desired by even the most pathologically individualistic people.

I have therefore adopted the alternative solution, which is to accept public goods on their own terms, to recognize that they must be provided in a different way from private goods and to investigate the implications of this problem of provision.

We have seen that, in certain circumstances, the problem solves itself, without any 'privatization' of the good in question. This happens in two main types of case. In the first place, public goods may be such that they involve the unanimous cooperation of the group of consumers if they are to be produced at all. We saw that a secret might have this property. In the age of nuclear weapons, it might well be that freedom from nuclear war also fits the description: if any single relevant decision-maker risks the destruction of the entire planet by his or her action, such action becomes considerably less likely (although *irrational* decision-makers are still, of course, liable to upset the global apple-cart). The more closely the number of people required to enable the production of a public good approximates to the size of the entire group of consumers, the more likely is this solution, although, as we saw when discussing anarchy, the potential for *any* free-riding at all makes the situation considerably more complex.

In the second place, public goods may arise as 'side-effects' of private goods provision. Thus, if people keep their own drains clean, public health may be enhanced. This possibility may result in the fortuitous provision of some public goods, but it is not clear that we could bank on being able to produce all of the public goods we want in this manner. This is not least because many of the external effects of private consumption are public bads, and an important class of public goods will involve the reduction of these. We saw later, when discussing public entrepreneurs, that one critical public good is, however, produced in this way. That good is competition between entrepreneurs, which produces an increase in the level of surplus available for retention by all consumers, whether or not they contribute to any of the costs of increased competition. No one sets out to provide competition *per se*, in either a public or private goods market, but a consequence of private maximizing activity by the participants in this market is something which is clearly a public good, and valuable to the entire group.

Despite the fact that the collective action problem solves itself in these two important cases, we saw that many public goods will not fall into these categories. Since we are not prepared to consider solutions either involving 'privatizing' the goods or depending upon philanthropists, philosopher-kings or other goody-goodies, we are forced to look for more political solutions.

At this stage, it is worth emphasizing another important distinction between different types of public good. Some will be tangible goods which actually have to be produced, while others will be less tangible and dependent on the modification of people's behaviour. The prevention of epidemics, for example, may be assisted both by people washing their hands before they touch other people's food and by the use of complex and expensive screening equipment. The good provided by hand-washing involves people in modifying their behaviour and doing something which is a bit of a nuisance. The good provided by the screening equipment involves a much more tangible collective effort and investment.

This distinction becomes significant when we consider the political, but stateless, solution to the problem provided by anarchy. As Taylor states them, anarchistic arrangements usually seem to involve some form of enlightened self-restraint. The goods which he suggests can be produced anarchistically are usually benefits which arise as a result of people behaving one way, when a narrower conception of self-interest suggests another. It seems to me that this is no accident, but happens because it is this type of good which is most susceptible to anarchistic provision. I am not sure whether there is anything intrinsic to the nature of the goods which makes this so, but it seems firstly to be the case that the modification of behaviour can be reversed more easily than the investment of more tangible resources, and secondly that goods involving the modification of behaviour require more near-unanimous cooperation than those involving investment. The second point is perhaps the more straightforward. Goods requiring self-restraint, for example, can more often be destroyed by the activity of a few wildcats. Freedom from nuclear war is the best example, but freedom from disease, pollution or other ills, and the preservation of natural resources also illustrate the point. It is often simply not worth modifying your behaviour if a few others are not doing the same thing. The more near-unanimous is the cooperation required, the closer is the collective action problem to solving itself. Goods involving investment, on the other hand, almost never *require* the cooperation of the entire group. Provided that the good generates a surplus for some individuals, those people could always make up a short-fall created by some free-riders. In this knowledge, free-riding is made more likely, and the conditional cooperation upon which anarchistic arrangements are based is made more unstable.

The *conditional* nature of the cooperation required lies at the root of the other difference between behaviour modification and investment. It seems to be easier for people to get 'locked in' to investment than to behavioural adjustments. Having changed your behaviour, it is rarely that difficult to change it back, leaving you no worse than you were before you started. Collective investments are rather different. Even remembering that economic man does not cry over spilt milk, you may be faced with the fact that, having spilt the milk, things are not quite the same. A project, which might not have been worth undertaking at all if everyone did not participate, might be worth continuing with if people back out halfway through. There might, for example, be costs in winding the project up once started, but, even if there are not, it might be the case that the contribution already made by the free-riders makes it worthwhile to continue. You end up paying more than they do for the same good, but it may still be worth it to you. For obvious reasons, conditional cooperation will be undermined if this is the case, and the anarchistic arrangements we have discussed will be less satisfactory. The fact that you can be suckered into a project by potential free-riders may well lead you to want firmer guarantees of continuing cooperation than conditional agreements can provide.

This type of anarchy, then, seems most suited to the modification of behaviour, which suggests that it might usefully be considered in relation to norms, since the modification of behaviour is what norms are all about. Thus, even in large and complex societies which do not fulfil the preconditions for Taylor's anarchy, it may be of considerable value in helping us to understand the observation of norms which cannot be effectively enforced by governments or other agencies. In this sense, much of our informal social life is anarchistic already. (The other important area of application is to those situations where coercive enforcement is, for one reason or another, not possible. These include international relations and the criminal underworld.)

It is clear that some public goods will elude anarchistic provision, yet be susceptible to provision, at a profit, by public entrepreneurs. The fact that I have devoted more space to this alternative should not be taken to imply that I regard it as more important (although it is more closely related to that which people conventionally think of as politics). The problem is that the issues involved here are more complex, mainly because we are forced to confront a new version of the collective action problem when trying to explain why people vote. Indeed, it is almost certainly true that there are as many public goods which are better provided anarchistically as there are which will tempt entrepreneurs. Goods involving the modification of behaviour, for example, yield no *direct* entrepreneurial surplus, while goods involving investment do. This does not mean that entrepreneurs cannot enforce norms, but it does mean that they must then also find a way of charging for their services. This will involve convincing people that they should pay for things which they would get for nothing if they cooperated, and will sometimes be difficult. For investment goods, people are in the business of paying anyway.

We saw that the ability of public entrepreneurs to produce collective consumption goods at a profit depends critically upon the use of sanctions to enforce some system of taxation. Thus, coercive revenue-gathering is what distinguishes public entrepreneurs from private entrepreneurs, and it has a number of extremely important consequences.

In the first place, rational individuals will never grant such coercive powers unconditionally, and they will never grant the power to coerce the whole group *en masse*. These restrictions are based upon the assumption that entrepreneurs are rational too, and mean that rational man would never voluntarily submit himself to a Hobbesian sovereign. (Hobbesian man is an even more depressing creature than rational man, being covetous and proud, and therefore has little choice.) Once more, therefore, we see the collective action problem 'solved' by the use of conditional agreements, this time between the population and an entrepreneur.

In the second place, the need to finance public goods on the basis of coercive powers of taxation has the effect of encouraging competition on the basis of sequential fixed-term monopoly rather than simultaneous provision. Entrepreneurs simultaneously in possession of coercive powers of taxation would probably compete in rather destructive ways. The effects of this need for monopoly rather than simultaneous provision permeate the rest of the argument, since they lie at the root of the tendency for the policies both of parties and of coalitions to converge on some lowest common denominator of electoral preference. Obviously, when people can be excluded from consuming goods, then they can be simultaneously provided, and a diversity of preference can be accommodated, just as it can in the market for purely private goods. When monopoly, even fixed-term monopoly, is called for, however, because recalcitrants cannot be excluded, the good in question cannot be provided in such a diverse form. In a competitive system, because there is only one government and only one public goods package enacted, the formulation of this package will tend to follow the lines of least resistance. This manifests itself either in a convergence of the policies on offer to the electorate or, if entry costs for entrepreneurs are low and a variety of packages are on offer, in a convergence on the centre ground by the coalitions which follow the election.

The principal factors which constrain this tendency for policies to converge stem from the other main source of revenue for entrepreneurs. While taxation is essential to entrepreneurs, additional income may be derived from the private suppliers of the factors of production of public goods. The income provides a crucial link between private and public goods markets to the extent that public goods are assembled from components which are themselves private goods, and to the extent that public policy will have implications for private producers. Our consideration of the calculus of voting problem showed that a voter's decision to turn out, if it is rational at all, is relatively marginal. Given the low expectations, costs must be low or voting will not be worth it. Furthermore, voters will economize on costs by making their decisions as easily as possible, on the basis of all sorts of cheap cues which are available. All of this makes voters susceptible to campaign expenditure. It also means that parties may increase their vote, not only by the policies they offer, but also by the campaign expenditure they involve themselves in. Modifying policy affects the potential vote; spending campaign funds transforms the potential vote into an actual vote. Thus, less popular policies can be compensated by more campaign expenditure. Participants in the private goods market, on the other hand, have an incentive to contribute towards parties' campaign funds only to the extent that this contribution produces some sort of effect. If they did not contribute, the party would simply have to offer the most popular policy. Thus, contributions from the private goods market will tend to produce less popular policies, and restrict the ideological convergence which will otherwise take place.

This is pretty much where we get. We start with rational man and public goods, and we end with two, possibly coexistent, modes of provision: 'anarchy' and 'entrepreneurs'. Anarchy tends to work with small groups and with goods involving the modification of behaviour. Entrepreneurs can produce capital goods. The need for monopoly provision tends to create a convergence of the alternatives on offer, although this is constrained by the interaction between the public and private goods market.

Finally, I would like to comment upon the methodological style I have used throughout. In the Introduction, I laid great stress upon the role of deductive arguments and fundamental potential explanations. This explains why, throughout the book, I have been more concerned with what might happen than with what does happen. Realistically, of course, a pure deductive explanation cannot be sustained outside the realms of formal logic and some branches of molecular physics. Being perfectly honest, I could not hold my head up and swear that I simply pulled a set of core assumptions out of a hat and just went on to unfold their implications. No one would believe me anyway. Obviously, the assumptions I have been working with are largely lifted straight from the many authors of rational choice theories. These authors got their assumptions from somewhere, and it was not out of a hat. When it comes to actually constructing theoretical arguments, the distinction between inductivism and deductivism is by no means clear-cut. The initial assumptions of most deductive arguments are obviously based on the observation of reality, so that some sort of back-street induction is really taking place. I hope I have shown to all but the most fundamentalist of theorists, however, that this back-street induction does not destroy the intellectual advantages of fundamental potential explanations and deductive logic. In practice, what we do is get our assumptions from somewhere, anywhere, try and make them as plausible as possible and *stick with them*. Fiddling around with assumptions when the going gets tough is what produces rationalizations rather than theories. Sticking with your assumptions for better or for worse may produce some funny-looking results. The hope is that some of them are also interesting.

Appendix: Theory and Practice

It should by now be quite clear that I do not regard the empirical validity of the theoretical arguments explored in this book to be a crucial issue. Nonetheless, the assumptions used do have some basis in reality, and the propositions they generate will clearly be more useful if they are more, rather than less, realistic. In this Appendix, therefore, I provide some brief notes on the ways in which we might generate testable propositions from the preceding argument.

CHAPTER 1   RATIONAL MAN

(a) The assumption of rationality

The basic assumption of rationality is almost certainly stated too generally at this stage to be capable of any sensible testing. The set of goals which may be desired is left completely unconstrained, and it is difficult to see how any behaviour could authoritatively be defined as irrational. The one exception to this is the individual who says, 'I prefer A to B. Therefore I choose B.' If there were too many people like this around, it would give us some cause for concern, although behaviour as systematically perverse as this would itself suggest something quite close to rationality. This assumption only acquires a cutting edge when it is considered in conjunction with the distinction between instrumental and intrinsic goals and with the statement that only individualistically defined goals may be intrinsically valued. (This is why I regard the fundamental potential explanation, or something rather like it, to be central to the usefulness of rational choice theory.)

(b) Socially defined goals may not be intrinsically valued

This is the most important assertion in the entire argument. As I have indicated, it is a constraint which can make rational choice theory more than a trivial exercise in the manipulation of truisms. While it is a very strong statement, and in principle susceptible to testing, it is also very general. We need to define our terms more carefully before we proceed.

'Socially defined goals' may be thought of as any goals which make no sense when attributed to an individual living in complete isolation from all others. A socially defined goal is thus a goal which requires reference to more than one individual in its definition.

'Intrinsically valued goals' are those for which there is no instrumental justification. A goal which is purely intrinsically valued is thus valued absolutely in itself and for itself, rather than being valued because its realization assists in the realization of other goals.

Our proposition can now be stated more precisely, and in a form in principle susceptible to empirical analysis: 'each individual, i, in the group will possess a set of goals, G_i. G_i will contain two subsets: a set of goals which is socially defined, S_i, and a set of goals which is intrinsically valued, I_i. For every individual in the group, $S_i \cap I_i = \emptyset$.' In other words, there will be no goal which is both in S_i and I_i. This statement can be tested, since it can be falsified by the discovery of a goal which belongs to both S_i and I_i. As we might expect, this is easier said than done, since it is very difficult to establish that there is no instrumental justification for any goal in I_i. In practice, the way to proceed might be to look for the reasons why a given goal is valued. Any goal for which we can say, 'It is valued because of x or because of y', will be discarded (although we may use x and y as a useful starting-point for the next round of investigation). There will be some goals for which we will simply have to say, 'They are valued because they are valued.' If these goals require more than one individual for their definition, then we have falsified the position $S_i \cap I_i = \emptyset$. (If I am determined to wriggle out of this, I can almost certainly come up with some form of instrumental justification for almost anything. You will, however, have falsified the proposition to your own satisfaction, which is all that really matters.)

(c) *Goals are in short supply*

This proposition applies to both instrumental and intrinsic goals. It is probably the least controversial proposition in the book. It states that there is a set of goals which may be completely realized within a given environment, and that the set of goals desired by all inhabitants of this environment is not in it. It may be disproved for a given group by demonstrating that all the goals of each group member may simultaneously be realized absolutely.

(d) *Decision costs*

This is a matter not so much for testing as for empirical investigation. We have assumed that taking decisions involves costs. From this we deduce that some decisions, where the stakes are high, will be allocated more decision-making expenditure than others, where they are not. This can of course be tested, but I suspect that it is non-controversial. The interesting matter for study is precisely what those decision costs are, and how some costs, such as time, are traded off against others, such as physical resources. Such a study might, for example, compare consumer decisions in a selection of complicated product areas where broadly similar information was available. Comparing cars and boxes of matches, for example, we would expect to find consumers spending more time studying and acting upon test reports of cars than test reports of matches. But how much more time? We do not know very much about these trade-offs, yet they are crucial to at least one part of our argument. This is the point at which we deduce that voters' decisions to turn out must be rather marginal, and hence susceptible to campaign expenditure. If we wish to actually use this deduction, which is based upon the assumption of decision costs, we need to know how much time and energy people are prepared to devote to a rather small probability of influencing an election.

CHAPTER 2   PUBLIC GOODS AND MARKET FAILURE

(a) *The collective action problem*

The basic statement of the collective action problem is that people will not voluntarily contribute to goods which they can consume regardless. This conclusion is based upon the idea that rational man does not part with resources unless he gets something in return. This in turn means that evidence concerning the collective action problem can be assembled from rational attitudes to charity and other forms of altruism. The restrictions imposed in Chapter 1 mean that charitable acts cannot be valued in themselves, since they make no sense when defined in terms of an isolated individual. Rational charity must thus be instrumental, if it is not to provide a falsification of the proposition in 1(b) above.

A large number of people clearly contribute small sums to charities from which they can derive no conceivable benefit. On the other hand, Chapter 2 also showed us how norms might emerge – and such a norm could well be giving small sums to 'deserving' causes – and be observed, for instrumental reasons, by otherwise self-centred individuals. In this context, small donations to charity do not provide a significant counter-example with which to falsify our propositions about rational man. A small donation, of the level 'expected', might be given simply in order to avert the mild social pressure which would be provided by failing to adhere to the norm. (We would feel happier about this interpretation if higher levels of donation were more forthcoming in public collections, for example in bars where peer groups would monitor deviation, than in private collections, for example those solicited through the post.) Anyway, a willingness to part with small sums – possibly below the cost threshold of rational decision-making – would not solve the collective action problem, since providing for all desired public goods would be considerably more expensive.

Large public charitable donations also do not provide a significant counter-factual. The very publicity associated with these transactions leaves open the possibility of some instrumental purpose. A serious problem would be posed for our assumptions, however, if it was reasonably common for people to make anonymous donations of sums of money which were larger than that which is commonly regarded as the norm.

While an investigation of charitable donations does throw some light on the collective action problem, a more direct test would be to compare rates of payment of taxes which posed defaulters with different probabilities of detection and punishment. We would expect taxes which posed much lower probabilities of detection to be much more difficult to collect. Thus, the rate of payment is low for dog licences and licences to tape-record broadcast material, where the probabilities of detection are very low, higher for television licences, where the probability of detection is higher, and higher still for the payment of V.A.T. or sales taxes by shopkeepers, where the probability of detection is higher still. A significant counter-factual to the propositions in the collective action problem would be an example of people paying a tax which it was absolutely impossible to enforce because non-payment was undetectable.

(b) *Pure jointness of production*

The main exception to the collective action problem arises when the unanimous cooperation of the group is necessary, if the good is to be produced at all. This is a firm statement, and can be tested, although there may not be many goods which fit this description. An important class of goods which may have this property are norms, to which we will return below.

(c) *Anarchy*

The two main modifications to the anarchistic agreements suggested by Taylor were the propositions that conditional cooperation will be more likely in groups which must interact over the provision of a range of goods, rather than a single good, and that conditional cooperation will be more likely with the provision of goods involving the modification of behaviour rather than capital investment.

Both of these are rather general statements, although they can be tested. For the first, we would predict that public goods provision would be more likely to be coercive or non-existent in groups which just happened to be brought together over a single aspect of their social consumption. If we consider membership of trade unions, for example – one of Olson's main concerns in *The Logic of Collective Action* – we would predict that coercive methods of enforcing membership, such as the closed shop, would be more likely to be found in cities, where potential members may interact only at work, than in small towns, where potential members may also live in the same community and thus have to get along in other spheres of life.

Similarly, we would predict that coercive methods of provision will be more common in goods involving capital investment than in those involving behaviour modification. Indeed, a strong example of capital investment in a non-excludable good which was organized along anarchistic lines would throw considerable doubt upon this proposition.

(d) Norms

The rational interpretation of norms essentially depends upon the proposition that norms are observed because something nasty happens to defectors. Rational adherence to norms should thus decline as the prospect and costs of discovery decrease. Examples of adherence to norms when there was no chance of discovery and/or very low penalties for deviants would undermine this interpretation. For obvious reasons, this cannot be researched on an individual level, since if the investigator can detect deviation, then so can others. On an aggregate level, however, we would predict that the most stable norms would be those for which the probability of detecting deviants, and the penalty subsequently imposed, were both high. We would expect people to be more likely to engage in anti-social behaviour, such as dropping litter or picking rare wild flowers, when there was no one else around than when they were in a crowd. These acts are no less anti-social when conducted in private, and if people simply observed norms for the sake of it, or because they thought they were 'good things', then their behaviour would not be modified by the presence or absence of an audience.

CHAPTER 3   PUBLIC ENTREPRENEURS AND POLITICAL PARTIES

(a) Sources of revenue

The deduction that taxation will be the principal source of revenue for public entrepreneurs depends upon the prior deduction that people will not voluntarily contribute significant sums for the production of goods which do not provide them with exclusive personal benefits. The testing of this deduction has just been discussed.

The second source of revenue for public entrepreneurs is the pool of private suppliers of the factors of production of public goods, and the other individuals whose *private* goods-maximizing activity is significantly affected by public policy. We should therefore look for examples of this type of donation, and further expect that such instrumental support would constitute the only source of revenue which, firstly, incumbents receive on a non-coercive basis and, secondly, challengers receive at all.

Significant contributions to challengers which had no personal instrumental motivation (in terms of their probable effects on public policy) would constitute worrying counter-examples. As a corollary of this, we would expect that challengers who clearly had no chance of influencing policy – either by becoming incumbents themselves, or by influencing incumbents to modify policy – should receive a much lower volume of contributions from these sources than those who had a clearer chance of success.

(b) *Sequential monopoly versus simultaneous provision*

Our consideration of the nature of competition for public goods contracts suggests that we should not find competitive simultaneous provision of those public goods which were not susceptible to the exclusion of free-riders. If we were to come up with a significant category of counter-examples to this proposition, then this would present a number of problems for the analysis, suggesting either that the collective action problem had alternative resolutions, or that entrepreneurs used sanctions in a more restrained fashion than we have assumed.

(c) *Collusion*

Unfortunately, although the propositions concerning collusion between politicians are some of the more interesting in the analysis, they are among the least susceptible to empirical investigation, since most forms of collusive behaviour are both secretive and flexible. Indeed, as soon as one type of collusion becomes capable of investigation, it is likely to be replaced by another. At this stage, therefore, we can probably proceed no further, although we will return to some aspects of this when discussing party competition.

CHAPTER 4   THE LOGIC OF VOTING

(a) *The calculus of voting problem*

The solution to this problem depended upon the assumption that voting costs are small, relative to the expected benefits, and the consequent deduction that voters' decisions are rather marginal. This implies that the level of voting will be quite sensitive to small changes in the costs and benefits, a proposition which may be tested. There is some evidence to suggest that the closeness of the contest in a constituency, the weather, the level of campaign expenditure by the parties and so on, affect the turn-out.[1] Although the proposition has not been systematically tested in this form, such evidence as there is suggests that the effect of these factors, although noticeable, is slight. Thus, while turn-out is lower in safe seats than in marginal ones, it is not very much lower; while bad weather does reduce voting levels, it does not decimate them, and so on. This lends weight to the possibility that electors are satisficing, rather than maximizing, when they vote, stripping decision costs to the minimum to match low expectations. Such very low costs (and voters' ability to reduce them when expectations are low) would make turn-out rather less sensitive to changes in costs and benefits, although these costs and benefits would still have some effect.

We are not now in a position to conduct a strong test of these propositions, since a number of interpretations can be generated from the same approach which are consistent with alternative versions of reality. The only strong statement we can make is that, if turn-out levels *increase* with increasing voting costs or decreasing benefits, then we have considerable cause for concern.

(b) *Deciding how to vote*

Some testing of the proposition that voters actually cast their vote in a manner consistent with a transitive preference ordering has already been conducted, using data from Northern Ireland.[2] Here, the Single Transferable Vote electoral system actually requires voters to express preference orderings, which can be partially uncovered by analysing vote transfers. If some distribution of electoral preference with respect to the policies advocated by the parties is assumed – and in Northern Ireland, such assumptions are relatively uncontroversial – it can be shown that voters did indeed behave according to the dictates of rationality. Overall, about 90 per cent of vote transfers went to parties specified by propositions generated from the assumption of voter rationality, and 5 per cent went to the more numerous group of other parties (5 per cent became non-transferable).[3]

In most countries, the electoral system is rather less helpful in this particular respect, and even quite complex survey techniques can enable the testing only of rather weaker propositions. On balance, however, such evidence as there is seems to suggest that it is easier to explain what people do when they are in the polling booth in rational terms than it is to explain how they got there in the first place. This empirical result corresponds with the status of the deductive model, which is probably at its weakest when tackling the calculus of voting problem.

CHAPTER 5   THE LOGIC OF PARTY COMPETITION

The principal conclusions in this chapter relate to the various ways in which party policy might deviate from that which would be indicated by straightforward maximization of the potential vote.

(a) *The effects of campaign expenditure*

Throughout this chapter, a distinction was made between the actual and the potential levels of support for politicians and parties. The assumption was made that, for the reasons discussed in Chapter 4, the level of campaign expenditure by a political party affects that party's ability to transform potential into actual support. The sensitivity of partisan support to campaign expenditure thus becomes a significant matter for empirical investigation. The problem, of course, is that, while actual support is easy to assess, potential support is not. Some evidence may be inferred by relating deviations between last-minute opinion-poll findings and actual voting figures to expenditure by parties designed to reduce voting costs (by providing transport to the polling-booth, reminding non-voters to turn out and so on). This will only tap a very limited part of the process, however, since the major part of parties' effort in campaigns is concerned with bombarding voters with free information and generally 'helping' them with their decision costs. We can never tell what the decision would have been had such campaign expenditure not been incurred, and are thus forced back into much more general statements like, 'In the long run, parties which spend more on campaigns will do better than parties which spend less.' There is some evidence to suggest that this is the case.[4]

If campaign expenditure does affect the transformation of potential into actual support, we saw that it should have an effect on party policy. This assumes that the sources of campaign funds do not have the same preferences as the electorate. In this case, we predict that deviations from policies which maximize potential support will be in the direction of the policies preferred by sponsors. We also predict that, the higher the level of campaign spending, the greater the possibility for deviation. Within the policy packages put forward by parties, we would expect those aspects which were unpopular to be the result of policy modifications necessary to please sponsors. In all of this, the underlying popularity of packages can probably be assessed only with the aid of surveys, however imperfect a tool these are, since each proposition relates to potential as opposed to actual support.

(b) Barriers to entry and party policy

The general conclusion that all barriers to entry into the system of party competition will reduce the ideological diversity of the packages on offer has a number of specific consequences. Ideological diversity should be affected by the electoral system, other restrictive aspects of electoral law and the level of 'break-in' competition costs. We would thus expect, other things being equal, greater diversity, *for the same number of parties*, in countries with more proportional electoral systems, with other restrictions (such as 5 per cent minimum vote shares before representation) and with high levels of campaign expenditure. These propositions may be difficult to investigate, but changes in the electoral system in a given country will provide particularly useful test cases. Comparing different two-or three-party systems, one consequence we would expect is that those with P.R. or low campaign expenditure would be more likely to deviate from that degenerate ideological convergence on the centre ground which is expected in those systems where the possibility of new parties can be discounted.

(c) Politicians' policy preferences

We concluded that party policy is most likely to deviate from the preferences of its members in two-party systems where either party stands a reasonable chance of success. In multi-party systems or in systems dominated by a single party, the chances of capturing or sharing in the incumbency are less directly related to vote-maximization and we can expect some deviation from vote-maximizing policies in the direction of the private preferences of the politicians concerned.

Given the measures of bargaining power provided, for example, by Shapley and Shubik, it should be possible to calculate, for a given situation, the increase in votes (and the source of that increase) which is most likely to increase bargaining power.[5] The greater the increase needed, the greater the likelihood of deviations from popular policies. The most obvious examples are those where a single party controls a vast majority of support, or three parties are evenly balanced. In each case, huge increases in voting strength are necessary to increase bargaining power, and we would expect parties' policies to come much closer to their members' preferences than when the competitive balance is much more critical.

CHAPTER 6 COALITIONS

Many of the basic principles of coalition theory have already been tested.[6] One matter discussed in this Chapter does remain open to useful empirical investigation, however. It was assumed, when discussing the importance of coalition bargaining on party policy, that parties will lose votes for going into coalition governments which enact policies differing significantly from those promised at the previous election. The extent to which this is indeed the case needs to be tested, and this can be achieved in a relatively straightforward manner.

Overall, however, coalition theory is distinguished by its considerable predictive success. This is probably because the assumptions of rational choice theory are at their best when applied to small numbers of highly motivated, calculating and well-informed actors. Indeed, I would not be at all surprised if, were systematic testing of the whole approach possible, it emerged in a much more favourable light in these situations than in those involving mass behaviour. This should not be taken to imply that mass behaviour is necessarily irrational; more that, when there are lots of people involved, the benefits are likely to be sufficiently small that the complex decisions necessary to conduct a rational calculus are simply not worthwhile. Faced with a small number of opponents, it is worth trying to win; faced with a vast group of them, rational man may simply have to make the best of a bad job.

Notes

INTRODUCTION

1. See Downs (1957) and Riker and Ordeshook (1973).

2. See Nozick (1974) and Rawls (1972).

3. Nozick (1974), p. 9.

CHAPTER 1

1. See, for example, Riker and Ordeshook (1973).

2. See, for example, Riker and Ordeshook (1973).

3. The seminal articles on this distinction are Samuelson (1954, 1958).

4. Samuelson (1954), p. 387.

5. The continuum representing 'publicness of consumption' was suggested, among others, by Buchanon (1965).

6. 'Jointness of supply' and 'excludability' form part of Samuelson's original definition (although he sees these properties as discrete rather than continuous). 'Optionality' and 'crowding' are discussed, among others, by Riker and Ordeshook (1973).

7. Readers should note that there are various, slightly different, definitions of 'jointness of supply'.

8. The seminal statement of this problem in a political context can be found in Olson (1965).

CHAPTER 2

1. Olson (1965), pp. 36–43.

2. See Laver (1976a), pp. 470–71.

3. For a fuller discussion of this point see Buchanon (1965).

4. Hobbes (1976), p. 173.

5. *ibid.*, p. 173.

6. *ibid.*, pp. 176–7.

7. *ibid.*, pp. 178–9.

8. *ibid.*, p. 175.

9. Taylor (1976).

10. *ibid.*, pp. 89–93.

11. *ibid.*, pp. 61–2.

12. The original example appears in a paper published last century by William Forster Lloyd. This is reprinted in Hardin (1964).

13. Ullmann-Margalit (1977).

14. *ibid.*, p. 60.

15. *ibid.*, p. 13.

16. *ibid.*, p. 30.

17. Buchanon (1975), Chapter 8.

18. *ibid.*, pp. 132–3.

19. Ullmann-Margalit (1977), pp. 36–41.

CHAPTER 3

1. Summarized by Frohlich, Oppenheimer and Young (1971).

2. *ibid.*, pp. 32–6.

3. *ibid.*, pp. 36–40.

4. *ibid.*, pp. 40–41.

5. *ibid.*, pp. 41–2.

6. Hirschman (1970).

7. See Laver (1976a) for a fuller discussion of this point.

8. Frohlich, Oppenheimer and Young (1971), pp. 80–88.

9. The seminal statement of this problem can be found in Arrow (1951).

10. Sen (1966). Some authors have concentrated on the existence of a single dimension of choice along which all alternatives can be ranked by all members of the group (see Niemi, 1969). Others have concentrated on the need for 'single peaked' structures of preferences (see Black, 1958).

11. This comment applies in particular to nearly all authors of theories of party competition. See, for example, Downs (1957), Robertson (1976) and Riker and Ordeshook (1973).

12. See Laver (1976b and 1976c) for a discussion of this in the extreme case of Northern Ireland.

13. For a discussion of various methods of evaluating bargaining power, see Brams (1975). The power index used in the following example was suggested by Shapley and Shubik (1954).

14. Call the parties A, B, C, D, E. Obviously when each has a weight of one and acts individually, the symmetry of the situation indicates that each has the same proportion (i.e. $1/5$) of the total power. When D and E combine into a single actor (DE) with weight 2, there are 24 possible combinations. These are, with the pivotal actor underlined:

A	B	*C*	(DE)	B	A	*C*	(DE)	C	A	*B*	(DE)
A	B	*(DE)*	C	B	A	*(DE)*	C	C	A	*(DE)*	B
A	C	*B*	(DE)	B	C	*A*	(DE)	C	B	*A*	(DE)
A	C	*(DE)*	B	B	C	*(DE)*	A	C	B	*(DE)*	A
A	*(DE)*	B	C	B	*(DE)*	A	C	C	*(DE)*	A	B
A	*(DE)*	C	B	B	*(DE)*	C	A	C	*(DE)*	B	A

(DE)	*A*	B	C
(DE)	*A*	C	B
(DE)	*B*	A	C
(DE)	*B*	C	A
(DE)	*C*	A	B
(DE)	*C*	B	A

A pivots 4 out of 24
B pivots 4 out of 24
C pivots 4 out of 24
(DE pivots 12 out of 24

15. It is nevertheless possible for groups to *lose* power by combining.
For example, a group of 20 actors has divided into the following
units:

A(10) B(2) C(2) D(2) E(2) F(2)

If E and F combine into a single unit (EF), the power indices for the
whole configuration before and after fusion are as follows:

	Before	After		Before	After
A	2/3	3/5	E	1/15	}1/10
B	1/15	1/10	F	1/15	
C	1/15	1/10	Thus E and F have 2/15 of the power between
D	1/15	1/10	them before the fusion and 1/10 (less) of it after.

CHAPTER 4

1. Downs (1957).

2. *ibid.*, p. 36.

3. *passim.*

4. See, for example, Stokes (1966), Barry (1970), Riker and Ordeshook
(1973), Robertson (1976) and Ordeshook (1976).

5. Especially Ordeshook.

6. Downs (1957), pp. 266–71.

7. *ibid.*, p. 268.

8. Riker and Ordeshook (1973), p. 63.

9. There is a vast literature on party identification. Readers un-
acquainted with this could try Campbell *et al.* (1960, 1966) and
Budge *et al.* eds (1976).

10. Robertson (1976), Appendix II.

11. Hirschman (1970).

12. See Budge and Farlie (1977).

13. See, for example, Stokes (1966), Laver (1976b, 1976c), Rusk and Borre (1976) and Mauser and Freyssinet-Dominjon (1976).

CHAPTER 5

1. This is the position argued by Downs (1957) and most of his followers.

2. Downs (1957), Chapter 4.

3. See Niemi (1969) and Riker and Ordeshook (1973), pp. 105–6.

4. Hirschman (1970), Chapter 6 and Robertson (1976).

5. See Robertson (1976).

6. Hirschman (1970), pp. 69–72.

CHAPTER 6

1. See Riker (1962).

2. See Axelrod (1970) and De Swaan (1973) for two alternative formulations of this.

3. See Taylor (1972) and Taylor and Laver (1973) for the consequences of lexicographical ordering of the various criteria usually employed by coalition theorists.

4. See Riker (1962), to which all discussions of size criteria defer.

5. Axelrod (1970).

APPENDIX

1. See Taylor and Johnston (1979), pp. 305–31 for a review of this evidence.

2. See Laver (1976b), pp. 324–34.

3. *ibid.*, pp. 328–9.

4. See Taylor and Johnston (1979).

5. See Shapley and Shubik (1954).

6. See, for example, Taylor and Laver (1973) and De Swaan (1973).

References

ARROW, KENNETH (1951) *Social Choice and Individual Values*, New York, Wiley.

AXELROD, ROBERT (1970) *Conflict of Interest*, Chicago, Markham.

BARRY, BRIAN (1970) *Sociologists, Economists and Democracy*, London, Collier Macmillan.

BLACK, DUNCAN (1958) *The Theory of Committees and Elections*, Cambridge, Cambridge University Press.

BRAMS, STEPHEN (1975) *Game Theory and Politics*, New York, Free Press.

BUCHANON, JAMES (1965) 'An Economic Theory of Clubs', *Economica*, 32: 1–14.

  (1975) *The Limits of Liberty*, Chicago, University of Chicago Press.

BUDGE, IAN, and DENNIS FARLIE (1977) *Voting and Party Competition*, London, Wiley.

BUDGE, IAN, IVOR CREWE and DENNIS FARLIE, eds. (1976) *Party Identification and Beyond*, London, Wiley.

CAMPBELL, A., P. CONVERSE, W. MILLER and D. STOKES (1960) *The American Voter*, New York, Wiley.

  (1966) *Elections and the Political Order*, New York, Wiley.

DESWAAN, ABRAM (1973) *Coalition Theories and Cabinet Formations*, Amsterdam, Elsevier.

DOWNS, ANTHONY (1957) *An Economic Theory of Democracy*, New York, Harper & Row.

FROHLICH, NORMAN, JOE OPPENHEIMER and ORAN YOUNG 1971) *Political Leadership and Collective Goods*, Princeton, Princeton University Press.

HARDIN, GARRET, ed. (1964) *Population, Evolution and Birth Control*, San Francisco, Freeman.

HIRSCHMAN, ALBERT (1970) *Exit, Voice and Loyalty*, Cambridge, Mass., Harvard University Press.

HOBBES, THOMAS (1976) *Leviathan*, London, Fontana.

LAVER, MICHAEL (1976a) ' "Exit, Voice and Loyalty" Revisited: the Strategic Production and Consumption of Public and Private Goods', *British Journal of Political Science*, 6: 463–82.

(1976b) 'Strategic Campaign Behaviour for Electors and Parties: the Northern Ireland Assembly Election of 1973', in Budge *et al.*, eds. (1976).

(1976c) *The Theory and Practice of Party Competition*, London and Beverly Hills, Sage.

MAUGER, GARY and JAQUELINE FREYSSINET-DOMINJON (1976) 'Exploring Political Space: A Study of French Voters' Preferences', in Budge *et al.*, eds. (1976).

NIEMI, RICHARD (1969) 'Majority Decision-Making with Partial Unidimensionality', *American Political Science Review*, 63: 488–97.

NOZICK, ROBERT (1974) *Anarchy, State and Utopia*, Oxford, Basil Blackwell.

OLSON, MANCUR (1965) *The Logic of Collective Action*, Cambridge, Mass., Harvard University Press.

ORDESHOOK, PETER (1976) 'The Spatial Theory of Elections: a Review and Critique', in Budge *et al.*, eds. (1976).

RAWLS, JOHN (1972) *A Liberal Theory of Justice*, Oxford, Clarendon Press.

RIKER, WILLIAM (1962) *The Theory of Political Coalitions*, New Haven, Yale University Press.

RIKER, WILLIAM, and PETER ORDESHOOK (1973) *An Introduction to Positive Political Theory*, New York, Prentice Hall.

ROBERTSON, DAVID (1976) *A Theory of Party Competition*, London, Wiley.

RUSK, J. and O. BORRE (1976) 'The Changing Party Space in Danish Voter Perceptions', in Budge *et al.*, eds. (1976).

SAMUELSON, PAUL (1954) 'A Pure Theory of Public Expenditure', *The Review of Economics and Statistics*, 36: 387–9.

(1958) 'Aspects of Public Expenditure Theories', *The Review of Economics and Statistics*, 40: 332–6.

SEN, AMARTYA (1966) 'A Possibility Theorem on Majority Decisions', *Econometrica*, 34: 491–9.

SHAPLEY, L., and M. SHUBIK (1954) 'A Method for Evaluating and Distribution of Power in a Committee System', *American Political Science Review*, 48: 787–92.

STOKES, DONALD (1966) 'Spatial Models of Party Competition', in Campbell *et al.*, eds. (1966).

TAYLOR, MICHAEL (1972) 'On the Theory of Government Coalition Formation', *British Journal of Political Science*, 2: 361–73.

TAYLOR, MICHAEL, and MICHAEL LAVER (1973) 'Government

Coalitions in Western Europe', *European Journal of Political Research*, 1: 205–48.

(1976) *Anarchy and Cooperation*, London, Wiley.

TAYLOR, P. J., and R. J. JOHNSTON (1979) *The Geography of Elections*, Harmondsworth, Penguin Books.

ULLMANN-MARGALIT, EDNA (1977) *The Emergence of Norms*, Oxford, Clarendon Press.

Index

More About Penguins
and Pelicans

For further information about books available from Penguins please write to Dept EP, Penguin Books Ltd, Harmondsworth, Middlesex UB7 0DA.

In the U.S.A.: For a complete list of books available from Penguins in the United States write to Dept CS, Penguin Books, 625 Madison Avenue, New York, New York 10022.

In Canada: For a complete list of books available from Penguins in Canada write to Penguin Books Canada Ltd, 2801 John Street, Markham, Ontario L3R 1B4.

In Australia: For a complete list of books available from Penguins in Australia write to the Marketing Department, Penguin Books Australia Ltd, P.O. Box 257, Ringwood, Victoria 3134.

In New Zealand: For a complete list of books available from Penguins in New Zealand write to the Marketing Department, Penguin Books (NZ) Ltd, P.O. Box 4019, Auckland 10.

By the same author

PLAYING POLITICS

This is a book of games, and a book about politics. It is for
anyone interested in politics, or who likes playing games – or
who thinks the two are synonymous anyway. It is intended
also as a useful adjunct for both teachers and students of
politics, adding a practical, constructive but enjoyable
dimension to their studies.

It is about getting your own say, seizing power, making
money, reneging on your promises. Players can be politicians,
form parties, fight elections, overthrow governments and make
all kinds of deals. From 'Primitive Politics' to 'Rolling Logs'
and from 'Elections' to 'Agenda', each game is an attempt to
capture the cut and thrust of political double-dealing.

CAPITAL

Volumes I, II and III

(*Volume I translated by Ben Fowkes, Volumes II and III translated by David Fernbach, and introduced by Ernest Mandel*)

Karl Marx/Friedrich Engels

THE COMMUNIST MANIFESTO

With an Introduction by A.J.P. Taylor

The complete text of the political tract which has exercised so great an influence on the world in the past century.

In a special introduction to this new edition A.J.P. Taylor charts the progress of the *Manifesto* from persecuted obscurity to global reverence and examines the relevance of Marx's nineteenth-century ideas to the realities of modern politics.